75 MAIN MEALS

75 MAIN MEALS

A CLASSIC COLLECTION OF FABULOUS AND VERSATILE
IDEAS TO COOK FOR EVERY OCCASION, SHOWN
STEP BY STEP IN OVER 300 PHOTOGRAPHS

LINDA FRASER

HERMES
HOUSE

This edition is published by Hermes House, an imprint of Anness Publishing Ltd,
Hermes House, 88–89 Blackfriars Road, London SE1 8HA;
tel. 020 7401 2077; fax 020 7633 9499
www.hermeshouse.com; www.annesspublishing.com

If you like the images in this book and would like to investigate using them for publishing, promotions or advertising,
please visit our website www.practicalpictures.com for more information.

Publisher: Joanna Lorenz
Senior Cookery Editor: Linda Fraser
Designers: Tony Paine and Roy Prescott
Photographers: Steve Baxter, Karl Adamson and Amanda Heywood
Food for Photography: Wendy Lee, Jane Stevenson and Elizabeth Wolf Cohen
Props Stylists: Blake Minton and Kirsty Rawlings
Additional recipes: Carla Capalbo and Laura Washburn

ETHICAL TRADING POLICY

Because of our ongoing ecological investment programme, you, as our customer, can have the pleasure and reassurance of knowing
that a tree is being cultivated on your behalf to naturally replace the materials used to make the book you are holding.
For further information about this scheme, go to www.annesspublishing.com/trees

Previously published as *Main Meal Dishes*

ACKNOWLEDGEMENTS

For their assistance in the publication of this book the publishers wish to thank:
Kenwood Appliances plc, New Lane, Havant, Hants P09 2NH
Prestige, Prestige House, 22–26 High Street, Egham, Surrey TW20 9DU
Magimix, 115A High Street, Godalming, Surrey GU7 1AQ
Le Creuset, The Kitchenware Merchants Ltd, 4 Stephenson Close, East Portway, Andover, Hampshire SP10 3RU

NOTES

For all recipes, quantities are given in both metric and imperial measures and, where appropriate, in standard cups and spoons.
Follow one set of measures, but not a mixture, because they are not interchangeable.

Standard spoon and cup measures are level. 1 tsp = 5ml, 1 tbsp = 15ml, 1 cup = 250ml/8fl oz.

Australian standard tablespoons are 20ml. Australian readers should use 3 tsp in place of 1 tbsp for measuring small quantities.

American pints are 16fl oz/2 cups. American readers should use 20fl oz/2.5 cups in place of 1 pint when measuring liquids.

Electric oven temperatures in this book are for conventional ovens. When using a fan oven, the temperature will probably need to be reduced
by about 10–20°C/20–40°F. Since ovens vary, you should check with your manufacturer's instruction book for guidance.

Medium (US large) eggs are used unless otherwise stated.

The apple symbol indicates a low fat, low cholesterol recipe.

CONTENTS

PREPARING MEAT FOR COOKING

Whether quickly grilled or stir-fried, or long-simmered for a rich flavour, meat lends itself to endless variety. Here, we give you the preparation tips and techniques that make meat cooking simplicity itself. Although you can buy meat ready for cooking from butchers and supermarkets, some cuts need further preparation, depending on how they are to be cooked.

HOW MUCH TO BUY

As a general guide, when buying boneless meat that has little or no fat, allow 145–200g/5–7oz per serving. For meat with bone that has a little fat at the edge, allow about 225g/8oz per serving. Very bony cuts such as shin and spareribs have proportionally little meat so you will need 450g/1lb per serving.

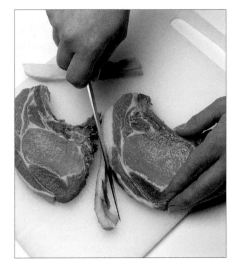

1 **To trim**: use a sharp knife to trim skin or rind and fat from the surface. Leave a little fat on steaks to be grilled, and slash this fat at regular intervals to prevent the steak curling up during cooking. Joints to be roasted should retain a thin layer of fat about 3–5mm/⅛–¼in. Cut away the sinews and tough connective tissue.

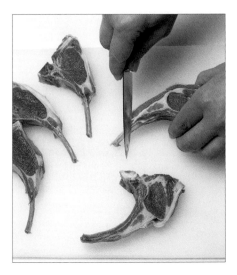

2 If you like, cut and scrape all fat and gristle from the ends of protruding bones (such as on cutlets or joints that contain rib bones). Cover the bone ends with foil to prevent charring.

3 **To chine a joint**: for large joints of meat that contain rib bones, such as rib of beef, pork loin and best end of lamb, it is a good idea to cut the chine bone where it is joined to the rib bones, to loosen it or to remove it completely before cooking. Do this with a meat saw and sharp knife or ask your butcher to do it. Without the chine bone, the joint will be easy to carve.

4 **To bard a joint**: if a very lean piece of meat is to be roasted without a protective crust (a spice mixture, oil and crumbs or pastry, for example), it is a good idea to bard it to keep it moist. Wrap very thin slices of beef fat, pork fat or blanched bacon around the joint and tie them in place. Discard the fat before serving but keep the bacon, if liked.

5 **To tie a boned joint**: joints that have been boned should be tied into a neat shape for roasting or pot roasting. The butcher will do this, but if you want to add a stuffing or seasoning, you will need to retie the joint yourself. Reshape it into a neat roll that is even in circumference. Use butcher's string to make ties around the circumference of the joint at 2.5cm (1in) intervals.

MINCING MEAT

Minced meats of all kinds are easily obtainable, but when you want something more unusual for a pâté or you want to use a particular cut of meat, well trimmed of gristle and tendons, you will mince it yourself. Also, if minced meat is to be served raw, as in steak tartare, it must be freshly prepared.

1 **With a mince**r: this produces the most uniform minced meat, and you can choose coarse or fine textures, according to which blade is used. Trim the meat well and cut it into 4 cm/1¼ in cubes or strips, then feed through the machine.

2 With a food processor: trim the meat carefully (be sure to remove all gristle because a food processor will chop gristle too) and cut it into cubes. Place in the machine fitted with the metal blade and pulse.

3 In between turning the machine on and off a few times, stir the meat around so that it is evenly minced. Care must be taken not to overprocess meat to a purée, particularly if making hamburgers.

4 **By hand**: trim the meat well. Using a large chef's knife, first cut the meat into cubes, then chop into smaller and smaller cubes. Continue chopping until you have the consistency you want, coarse or fine.

PREPARING ESCALOPES

Escalopes are slices of veal from the fillet end of the leg, cut ⅜ in (1 cm) thick. They need to be pounded before cooking, to break the fibres. This tenderizes them and helps to keep them flat during cooking. Slices of other meat or poultry may also be called escalopes. Beef slices cut from the top of the leg, to be rolled and braised are prepared in the same way.

POUNDING IT OUT

You can also use the base of a heavy saucepan or frying pan to pound and flatten meat escalopes. Choose a pan with a smooth base.

1 Trim any fat and gristle from around the edge of each escalope. Lay it flat between two sheets of cling film or greaseproof paper.

2 Using the smooth side of a meat mallet or the long side of a rolling pin, pound gently but firmly all over the escalope to flatten it to 3–5mm/ ⅛–¼in thickness. It will spread out to almost twice its original size.

ROASTING MEAT

The dry heat of oven roasting is best suited to tender cuts of meat. If they don't have a natural marbling of fat, bard them. Alternatively, marinate the meat or baste it frequently with the roasting juices during cooking.

Meat should be at room temperature for roasting. Roast on a rack in a tin that is just a little larger than the joint.

There are two methods of roasting meat. For the first, the joint is seared at a high temperature and then the heat is reduced for the remainder of the cooking time. For the second method, the joint is roasted at a constant temperature throughout.

1 According to the recipe, rub the joint with oil or butter and season. If wished, for extra flavour, with the tip of a sharp knife make little slits in the meat all over the surface. Insert flavourings such as herbs, slivers of garlic, olive slices, and so on.

2 Roast for the suggested time, basting if necessary. Transfer the cooked meat to a carving board. Leave it to rest for 10–15 minutes before carving. During this time, make a gravy with the roasting juices, if liked.

SUGGESTED ROASTING TIMES

Following the second roasting method, in a 180°C/350°C/Gas 4 oven, approximate timings in minutes per 450g 1lb:

    Beef, rare, 20 + 20 extra
        medium, 25 + 25 extra
        well done, 30 + 30 extra
    Veal, 25 + 25 extra
    Lamb, 25 + 25 extra
    Pork, 35 + 35 extra

(*Prime cuts such as rib of beef and tenderloin need less time.)

MEAT THERMOMETER READINGS			
Beef		**Lamb**	
rare	52–54°C/125–130°F	rare	54–57°C/130–135°F
medium-rare	57°C/135°F	medium	60–63°C/140–145°F
medium	60–63°C/140–145°F	well done	71°C/160°F
well done	71°C/160°F		
		Pork	
Veal		medium	66°C/150°F
well done	71°C/160°F	well done	71–74°C/160–165°F

TESTING TO DETERMINE WHEN MEAT IS COOKED

The cooking times given in a recipe are intended to be a guideline. The shape of a cut can affect how long it takes to cook, so testing is essential.

1 Large roasts can be tested with a metal skewer. Insert the skewer into the thickest part and leave it for 30 seconds. Withdraw the skewer and feel it: if it is warm, the meat is rare; if it is hot, the meat is well cooked.

2 The most reliable test is with the use of a meat thermometer, inserted in the centre of the joint, away from bones. See the chart for the internal temperatures.

NATURAL LAW OF ROASTING

A joint will continue to cook in its own retained heat for 5–10 minutes after being removed from oven or pot, so it is a good idea to take it out when it is just below the desired thermometer reading.

DEGLAZING FOR A PAN SAUCE

After pan-frying or sautéing, a simple yet delicious sauce can be made in the pan. The same method can be used to make gravy for roast meats. It is also a good way to maximize flavour in stews and casseroles.

Before deglazing, remove the meat and keep it warm. Pour or spoon off all the fat from the pan, unless the recipe calls for shallots, garlic, or the like to be softened. In that case, leave 5–10ml/ 1–2tsp of fat and cook the vegetables in it.

1 Pour in the liquid (wine, stock, vinegar, etc). Bring to the boil, stirring well to scrape up all the browned bits from the bottom of the pan.

2 Boil over a high heat for 1–2 minutes or until the liquid is almost syrupy. Add cream or butter if you like, then season to taste and serve.

MAKING GRAVY

Gravy made from the roasting juices is rich in flavour and colour. It is a traditional accompaniment for roast meat and poultry.

REST BEFORE CARVING

Once a joint is removed from the oven or pot, it should be left in a warm place to 'rest' for 10–15 minutes. During this time, the temperature of the joint evens out, and the flesh reabsorbs most of the juices.

1 Spoon off most of the fat from the roasting tin. Set the tin over moderately high heat, add flour and stir to combine well.

2 Cook, scraping tin well until it forms a smooth brown paste. Add stock or liquid and bring to the boil, stirring. Simmer, then season.

BROWNING OR SEARING MEAT

Meat is sometimes seared as the first step in its cooking. This may be done either by roasting briefly at a high temperature and then reducing the heat or by frying. The result is a browned crust that adds delicious flavour.

POT ROASTING

This method of cooking tenderizes even the toughest cuts of meat.

Meat to be pot-roasted may or may not have an initial searing.

1 **To sear by frying**: dry the meat well. Heat a little oil in a frying pan or flameproof casserole until very hot. Fry meat over high heat until well browned. Turn the meat using two spatulas or spoons.

2 If roasting, transfer the meat to the oven. If pot-roasting, add a small amount of liquid and cover the casserole tightly. If a frying pan has been used for searing, be sure to deglaze it (see above).

STIR-FRYING

The preparation of ingredients for stir-frying often takes longer than the cooking itself. This is because all ingredients must be cut to uniform sizes so that the cooking can be accomplished quickly and evenly.

A wok is excellent for stir-frying because its high sides let you stir and toss the ingredients briskly. Use long cooking chopsticks or a wooden spatula to keep the ingredients moving around the wok.

1 Prepare all the ingredients in uniformly sized pieces following recipe instructions.

2 Heat a wok or large deep frying pan over moderately high heat. Dribble in the oil down the sides.

3 When the oil is hot (a piece of vegetable should sizzle on contact), add the ingredients in the order specified in the recipe. (Those that take longer to cook are added first.) Do not add too much to the wok at a time or the ingredients will start to steam rather than fry.

4 Fry, stirring and tossing constantly with chopsticks or a spatula, until the ingredients are just cooked: vegetables should be crisp-tender and meat and poultry tender and juicy.

5 Push the ingredients to the side of the wok or remove them. Pour liquid or sauce as specified in the recipe into the bottom. Cook and stir, then mix in the ingredients from the side. Serve immediately.

PAN-FRYING AND SAUTÉING

Tender cuts of meat, such as steaks and chops, slices of calves' liver and hamburgers, are ideal for cooking quickly in a heavy frying pan. And the juices left in the pan can be turned into an easy sauce.

Before pan-frying and sautéing, trim excess fat from steaks, chops, escalopes, etc, then dry them very thoroughly with paper towels.

For cooking, use a fat that can be heated to a high temperature. If using butter, an equal amount of vegetable oil will help prevent burning.

1 Heat the fat in the pan over high heat until very hot but not browning. Put in the meat, in one layer. Do not crowd the pan.

2 Fry until browned on both sides and done to your taste. If pan-frying pork or veal chops, reduce the heat to moderate once they are in the pan.

MAKING MEAT STOCK

The most delicious meat soups, stews, casseroles, gravies and sauces rely on a good home-made stock for success. Neither a stock cube nor a canned consommé will do if you want the best flavour. Once made, meat stock can be kept in the refrigerator for four or five days, or frozen for longer storage (up to six months).

ON THE LIGHT SIDE

For a light meat stock, use veal bones and do not roast the bones or vegetables. Put in the pot with cold water and cook as described.

Makes about 2 litres/3½ pints

1.8kg/4lb beef bones, such as shin, leg, neck and clod, or veal or lamb bones, cut into 6cm/2½in pieces
2 onions, unpeeled, quartered
2 carrots, roughly chopped
2 celery sticks, with leaves if possible, roughly chopped
2 tomatoes, coarsely chopped
4.5 litres/7½ pints cold water
a handful of parsley stalks
a few fresh thyme sprigs or 5ml/1tsp dried thyme
2 bay leaves
10 black peppercorns, lightly crushed

1 Preheat a 230°C/450°C/Gas 8 oven. Put the bones in a roasting tin or flameproof casserole and roast, turning occasionally, for 30 minutes or until they start to brown.

2 Add the onions, carrots, celery and tomatoes and baste with the fat in the tin. Roast for a further 20–30 minutes or until the bones are well browned. Stir and baste occasionally.

3 Transfer the bones and vegetables to a stockpot. Spoon off the fat from the roasting tin.

4 Add a little of the water to the roasting tin or casserole and bring to the boil on top of the stove, stirring well to scrape up any browned bits. Pour this liquid into the stockpot.

5 Add the remaining water. Bring just to the boil, skimming frequently to remove all the foam from the surface. Add the parsley, thyme, bay leaves and peppercorns.

6 Partly cover the pot and simmer the stock for 4–6 hours. The bones and vegetables should always be covered with liquid, so top up with a little boiling water from time to time if necessary.

7 Strain the stock through a sieve. Skim as much fat as possible from the surface. If possible, cool the stock and then chill it; the fat will rise to the top and set in a layer that can be removed easily.

LIGHT LUNCHES

In the middle of the day meals need to be quick to prepare and eat. In this chapter there are plenty of speedy, yet delicious, recipes to choose from. There are rice dishes, noodles with prawns, tasty home-made burgers, a vegetarian bake made with chick-peas and artichokes, and several very simple, yet filling, pasta dishes to tempt you: try Tagliatelle with Hazelnut Pesto, if you use fresh pasta, it will be ready to serve in well under 10 minutes.

Kedgeree

Popular for breakfast in Victorian times, Kedgeree has its origins in *Khichri*, an Indian rice and lentil dish, and is often flavoured with curry powder.

INGREDIENTS

Serves 4

500g / 1¼lb smoked haddock
115g / 4oz / generous ½ cup long grain
    rice
30ml / 2 tbsp lemon juice
150ml / 5fl oz / ⅔ cup single or
    soured cream
pinch of freshly grated nutmeg
pinch of cayenne pepper
2 hard-boiled eggs, peeled and cut into
    wedges
50g / 2oz / 4 tbsp butter, diced
30ml / 2 tbsp chopped fresh parsley
salt and black pepper
parsley sprigs, to garnish

1 Poach the haddock, just covered by water, for about 10 minutes, until the flesh flakes easily. Lift the fish from the cooking liquid using a slotted spoon. Remove any skin and bones, then flake the flesh.

2 Pour the rice into a measuring jug and note the volume, then tip out, pour the fish cooking liquid into the jug and top up with water, until it measures twice the volume of the rice.

3 Bring the fish cooking liquid to the boil, add the rice, stir, then cover and simmer for about 15 minutes, until the rice is tender and the liquid absorbed. While the rice is cooking, preheat the oven to 180°C / 350°F / Gas 4, and butter a baking dish.

4 When the rice is cooked, remove from the heat and stir in the lemon juice, cream, flaked fish, nutmeg and cayenne. Add the egg wedges to the rice mixture and stir in gently.

5 Tip the rice mixture into the baking dish, dot with butter and bake for about 25 minutes.

6 Stir the chopped parsley into the Kedgeree, check the seasoning and garnish with parsley sprigs.

COOK'S TIP

Taste the Kedgeree before you add salt, since the smoked haddock may already be quite salty.

Noodles with Prawns in Lemon Sauce

As in many Chinese dishes the fish is here purely for colour and a little flavour. You could serve this noodle dish on its own, or with several others as part of a Chinese-style meal.

INGREDIENTS

Serves 4

2 packets Chinese egg noodles
15ml/1 tbsp sunflower oil
2 sticks celery, cut into
    matchsticks
2 garlic cloves, crushed
4 spring onions, sliced
2 carrots, cut into matchsticks
7.5cm/3in piece cucumber, cut into
    matchsticks
115g/4oz prawns in shells
1 lemon, or 30ml/2 tbsp lemon sauce
5ml/1 tsp cornflour
60–75ml/4–5 tbsp fish stock
115g/4oz/1 cup cooked, peeled prawns
salt and black pepper
few sprigs dill, to garnish

1 Put the noodles in boiling water and leave to soak as directed on the packet. Meanwhile, heat the oil in a pan and stir-fry the celery, garlic, spring onions and carrots for 2–3 minutes.

2 Add the cucumber and whole prawns and cook for 2–3 minutes. Meanwhile, peel the rind from the lemon and cut into long thin shreds. Place in boiling water for 1 minute.

3 Blend the lemon juice, or lemon sauce, with the cornflour and stock and add to the pan. Bring gently to the boil, stirring, and cook for 1 minute.

4 Stir in the shelled prawns, the drained lemon rind and seasoning to taste. Drain the noodles and serve with the prawns, garnished with dill.

— COOK'S TIP —

These noodles can also be deep-fried. Once cooked as above, drain on kitchen paper. Deep-fry small amounts at a time, until golden brown and very crisp.

Pasta Carbonara

An Italian favourite whose name translates as 'charcoal burners' pasta'. Traditionally made with spaghetti, it is equally delicious with fresh egg tagliatelle.

INGREDIENTS

Serves 4
350–450g/12oz–1lb fresh tagliatelle
15ml/1 tbsp olive oil
225g/8oz piece of ham, bacon or pancetta, cut into 2.5cm/1in sticks
115g/4oz (about 10) button mushrooms, sliced
4 eggs, lightly beaten
75ml/5 tbsp single cream
salt and black pepper
30ml/2 tbsp finely grated Parmesan cheese
fresh basil sprigs, to garnish

1 Cook the pasta in a pan of boiling salted water, with a little oil added, for 6–8 minutes or until *al dente*.

2 Meanwhile, heat the oil in a frying pan and add the ham. Fry for 3–4 minutes and then add the mushrooms and fry for a further 3–4 minutes. Turn off the heat and reserve. Lightly beat the eggs and cream together in a bowl and season well.

3 When the pasta is cooked, drain it well and return to the pan. Add the ham, mushrooms and any pan juices and stir into the pasta.

4 Pour in the eggs and cream and half the Parmesan cheese. Stir well and as you do this the eggs will cook in the heat of the pasta. Pile on to warmed serving plates, sprinkle with the remaining Parmesan and garnish with basil.

Baked Macaroni Cheese

A British supper-time dish – replace the Cheddar with your family's favourite cheese.

INGREDIENTS

Serves 4
15ml/1 tbsp olive oil
275g/10oz/2⅓ cups macaroni
2 leeks, chopped
50g/2oz/4 tbsp butter
50g/2oz/½ cup plain flour
900ml/1½ pints/3¾ cups milk
225g/8oz/2 cups grated mature Cheddar cheese
30ml/2 tbsp fromage frais
5ml/1 tsp wholegrain mustard
50g/2oz/1 cup fresh breadcrumbs
25g/1oz/½ cup grated Double Gloucester cheese
salt and black pepper
15ml/1 tbsp chopped fresh parsley, to garnish

1 Preheat the oven to 180°C/350°F/Gas 4. Bring a large pan of salted water to the boil and add the olive oil. Add the macaroni and leeks and boil gently for 10 minutes. Drain, rinse under cold water and reserve.

2 Heat the butter in a saucepan, stir in the flour and cook for about a minute. Remove from the heat and gradually add the milk, stirring well after each addition until smooth. Return to the heat and stir continuously until thickened.

3 Add the Cheddar cheese, fromage frais and mustard, mix well, and season with salt and pepper.

4 Stir the drained macaroni and leeks into the cheese sauce and pile into a greased ovenproof dish. Level the top with the back of a spoon and sprinkle over the breadcrumbs and Double Gloucester cheese.

5 Bake for 35–40 minutes. Serve hot, garnished with fresh parsley.

Pork and Celery Popovers

Lower in fat than they look, and a good way to make the meat go further, these little popovers will be popular with children.

INGREDIENTS 🍎

Serves 4
sunflower oil, for brushing
150g/5oz/1¼ cup plain flour
1 egg white
250ml/8fl oz/1 cup skimmed milk
120ml/4fl oz/½ cup water
350g/12oz lean minced pork
2 celery stalks, finely chopped
45ml/3 tbsp rolled oats
30ml/2 tbsp snipped chives
15ml/1 tbsp Worcestershire sauce
salt and black pepper

1 Preheat the oven to 220°C/425°F/ Gas 7. Brush 12 deep patty tins with a small amount of oil.

2 Place the flour in a bowl and make a well in the centre. Add the egg white and milk and gradually beat in the flour. Gradually add the water, beating until smooth and bubbly.

3 Place the minced pork, celery, rolled oats, chives, Worcestershire sauce, and seasoning in a bowl and mix well. Mould the mixture into 12 small balls and place in the patty tins.

4 Cook for 10 minutes, remove from the oven, and quickly pour the batter into the tins. Cook for 20–25 minutes more, or until puffed and golden brown. Serve hot with thin gravy and fresh vegetables.

—————— COOK'S TIP ——————

Transfer the batter to a jug so that you can easily and quickly divide it among the patty tins, then return to the oven at once – the tin must not be allowed to cool down or the popovers won't rise.

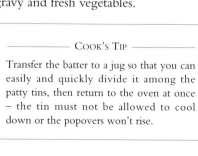

Cornish Pasties

There are many traditional recipes for pasties, which were the original packed lunch, but usually people just used to add whatever was available.

INGREDIENTS

Makes 6
500−675g/1¼−1½lb ready-made
  shortcrust pastry
450g/1lb chuck steak, diced
1 potato, about 175g/6oz, diced
175g/6oz swede, diced
1 onion, chopped
2.5ml/½ tsp dried mixed herbs
a little beaten egg, to glaze
salt and black pepper

1 Preheat the oven to 220°C/425°F/ Gas 7. Divide the pastry into six equal pieces, then roll out each piece to a 20cm/8in round.

2 Mix together the steak, vegetables, herbs and seasoning, then spoon an equal amount on to one half of each pastry round.

COOK'S TIP

Other vegetables, such as turnip, carrot or celery could be used in place of the swede, if you prefer.

3 Brush the pastry edges with water, then fold the free half of each round over the filling. Press the edges firmly together to seal.

4 Use a fish slice to transfer the pasties to a baking sheet, then brush each one with beaten egg.

5 Bake the pasties for 15 minutes, then reduce the oven temperature to 160°C/325°F/Gas 3 and bake for a further hour. Serve hot or cold.

Cauliflower Cheese

INGREDIENTS

Serves 4

1 cauliflower, broken into large florets
40g/1½oz/3 tbsp butter
1 small onion, chopped
2 slices streaky bacon, chopped
45ml/3 tbsp plain flour
450ml/¾ pint/scant 2 cups milk
115g/4oz/1 cup grated mature
   Cheddar cheese
pinch of English mustard powder
salt and pepper

1 Cook the cauliflower in boiling salted water until almost tender. Drain well and tip into a baking dish.

2 Meanwhile, melt the butter in a saucepan and gently cook the onion and bacon until the onion is soft, then spoon over the cauliflower.

3 Stir the flour into the butter in the pan and cook, stirring, for 1 minute. Remove the pan from the heat and slowly pour the milk into the pan, stirring all the time.

4 Return the saucepan to the heat and bring to the boil, stirring constantly. Simmer for 4–5 minutes, stirring occasionally.

5 Preheat the grill. Remove the pan from the heat and then stir in three-quarters of the cheese. Add the mustard and seasoning to taste.

6 Pour the cheese sauce over the cauliflower, then sprinkle the remaining cheese over the top and put under the grill until the top is golden and bubbling.

Golden Cheese Pudding

INGREDIENTS

Serves 4

600ml/1 pint/2½ cups milk
75g/3oz/1¾ cups fresh breadcrumbs
175g/6oz/1½ cups grated mature
   Cheddar cheese
7.5ml/1½ tsp prepared mustard
4 eggs, separated
salt and pepper

—— COOK'S TIP ——
When whisking egg whites, make sure that both the bowl and the beaters are clean and dry.

1 Bring the milk to the boil, then stir in the breadcrumbs.

2 Meanwhile, preheat the oven to 180°C/350°F/Gas 4 and butter a 1.5 litre/2½ pint/6¼ cup baking dish.

3 Whisk the egg whites in a large bowl until stiff but not dry, then carefully fold the egg whites into the breadcrumb mixture using a large spoon or a spatula in three batches.

4 Transfer the mixture to the baking dish and bake for about 30–45 minutes, depending on the depth of the dish, until just lightly set and golden.

Toad in the Hole

Sausages are cooked in a light batter which rises to a crisp, brown crust, making this a tasty and substantial supper dish.

INGREDIENTS

Serves 4

90g/3½oz/scant 1 cup plain
 flour
30ml/2 tbsp chopped fresh parsley
10ml/2 tsp chopped fresh thyme
1 egg, beaten
300ml/½ pint/1¼ cups milk and
 water, mixed
60ml/4 tbsp oil
450g/1lb good-quality sausages
salt

1 Stir the flour, chopped herbs and salt together in a bowl and form a well in the centre.

2 Pour the egg into the well, then gradually pour in the milk and water while stirring the dry ingredients into the liquids. Beat to form a smooth batter, then leave for 30 minutes.

3 Preheat the oven to 220°C/425°F/ Gas 7. Pour the oil into a small roasting tin or baking dish, add the sausages, turn them to coat them thoroughly in the oil, then cook the sausages in the oven for 10–15 minutes, until they are beginning to brown all over and the oil is very hot.

4 Stir the batter using a wooden spoon, then remove the roasting tin or baking dish from the oven and quickly pour the batter over the sausages and return the roasting tin or baking dish to the oven to bake for about 40 minutes (depending on the depth of the batter), until well risen and crisp around the edges.

COOK'S TIP

It is important to preheat the oil with the sausages so that the batter rises well and becomes crisp.

Beef and Mushroom Burgers

It's worth making your own burgers to cut down on fat – in these the meat is extended with mushrooms for extra fibre.

INGREDIENTS 🍎

Serves 4
1 small onion, chopped
150g/5oz/2 cups small cup mushrooms
450g/1lb lean minced beef
1 cup fresh wholemeal
   breadcrumbs
5ml/1 tsp dried mixed herbs
15ml/1 tbsp tomato purée
plain flour, for shaping
salt and black pepper

1 Place the onion and mushrooms in a food processor and process until finely chopped. Add the beef, bread-crumbs, herbs, tomato purée and seasonings. Process for a few seconds, until the mixture binds together but still has some texture.

2 Divide the mixture into 8–10 pieces, then press into burger shapes using lightly floured hands.

3 Cook the burgers in a non-stick frying pan, or under a hot grill for 12–15 minutes, turning once, until evenly cooked. Serve with relish and lettuce, in burger buns or pitta bread.

COOK'S TIP

The mixture is soft, so handle carefully and use a fish slice for turning to prevent the burgers from breaking during cooking.

VARIATION

To make Lamb and Mushroom Burgers, substitute lean minced lamb for the minced beef.

Bacon and Egg Bread Pudding

Bacon and egg is such an obvious combination, but perhaps not often thought of as a bread pudding. But it is delicious and could use up leftover ingredients.

INGREDIENTS

Serves 4

8 rashers bacon, crisply grilled, rinded and chopped
5–6 slices bread, buttered
2 eggs
300ml/½ pint/1¼ cups milk
1 garlic clove, crushed
50g/2oz/½ cup grated Cheddar cheese
salt and black pepper

1 Sandwich the bacon between the bread slices, cut into triangles and arrange in a buttered ovenproof dish.

2 Mix the eggs, milk and garlic, and season to taste. Pour over the bread and leave to soak up for about 10 minutes. Meanwhile, preheat the oven to 180°C/350°F/Gas 4.

3 Sprinkle the grated cheese over the top of the bread pudding and bake for 30–40 minutes, until golden brown. (Finish off under the grill if it needs further browning.)

Chick-peas and Artichokes au Gratin

For last-minute lunches this is a very quick, extremely tasty, and unusual dish.

INGREDIENTS

Serves 4

400g/14oz can chick-peas, drained
400g/14oz can blackeye beans, drained
137g/4½oz jar artichoke antipasti (or canned artichoke hearts, chopped, plus a little olive oil)
1 red pepper, seeded and chopped
1 garlic clove, crushed
15ml/1 tbsp chopped fresh parsley
5ml/1 tsp lemon juice
150ml/¼ pint/⅔ cup soured cream
1 egg yolk
50g/2oz/½ cup grated cheese
salt and black pepper

1 Preheat the oven to 180°C/350°F/ Gas 4. Mix the chick-peas, beans, artichoke antipasti or artichoke hearts, and red pepper together.

2 Stir in as much of the artichoke dressing, or oil if using artichoke hearts, as is necessary to moisten the mixture. Stir in the garlic, parsley, lemon juice and seasoning to taste.

3 Mix together the soured cream, egg yolk, cheese and seasoning. Spoon evenly over the vegetables and bake for 25–30 minutes, or until the top is golden brown.

Corned Beef and Egg Hash

This classic American hash is made with corned beef and is a popular brunch or lunchtime dish all over the United States. Serve with chilli sauce for a really authentic touch.

INGREDIENTS

Serves 4

30ml/2 tbsp vegetable oil
25g/1oz/2 tbsp butter
1 onion, finely chopped
1 small green pepper, seeded and diced
2 large boiled potatoes, diced
350g/12oz can corned beef, cubed
1.25ml/¼ tsp grated nutmeg
1.25ml/¼ tsp paprika
4 eggs
salt and black pepper
chopped fresh parsley, to garnish
sweet chilli sauce or tomato sauce,
   to serve

1 Heat the oil and butter together in a large frying pan and add the onion. Fry for 5–6 minutes, until softened.

2 In a bowl, mix together the pepper, potatoes, corned beef, nutmeg and paprika and season well. Add to the pan and toss gently to distribute the cooked onion. Press down lightly and fry on a medium heat for about 3–4 minutes, until a golden brown crust has formed on the bottom.

3 Stir the mixture through to distribute the crust, then repeat the frying twice, until the mixture is well browned.

4 Make four wells in the hash and crack an egg into each one. Cover and cook gently for about 4–5 minutes, until the egg whites are just set.

5 Sprinkle with chopped parsley and cut the hash into quarters. Serve hot with sweet chilli sauce.

—————— COOK'S TIP ——————

Pop the can of corned beef into the fridge to chill for about half an hour before using – it will firm up and cut into cubes more easily.

Beef Strips with Orange and Ginger

Stir-frying is one of the best ways to cook with the minimum of fat. It's also one of the quickest ways to cook, but you do need to choose tender meat.

INGREDIENTS 🍎

Serves 4

450g/1lb lean beef rump, fillet, or sirloin, cut into thin strips
finely grated rind and juice of 1 orange
15ml/1 tbsp light soy sauce
5ml/1 tsp cornflour
2.5cm/1in piece root ginger, finely chopped
10ml/2 tsp sesame oil
1 large carrot, cut into thin strips
2 spring onions, thinly sliced

1 Place the beef strips in a bowl and sprinkle over the orange rind and juice. If possible, leave to marinate for at least 30 minutes.

2 Drain the liquid from the meat and set aside, then mix the meat with the soy sauce, cornflour, and ginger.

COOK'S TIP

If you haven't any sesame oil, then use sunflower oil, or try flavoured chilli oil, or a nut oil such as hazelnut or walnut instead.

3 Heat the oil in a wok or large frying pan and add the beef. Stir-fry for 1 minute until lightly coloured, then add the carrot and stir-fry for another 2–3 minutes more.

4 Stir in the spring onions and reserved liquid, then cook, stirring, until boiling and thickened. Serve hot with rice noodles or plain boiled rice.

Tagliatelle with Hazelnut Pesto

Hazelnuts are lower in fat than other nuts, which makes them useful for this reduced-fat alternative to pesto sauce.

INGREDIENTS 🍎

Serves 4

2 garlic cloves, crushed
25g/1oz/1 cup fresh basil leaves
25g/1oz/¼ cup hazelnuts
200g/7oz/⅞ cup skimmed milk soft
  cheese
225g/8oz dried tagliatelle, or 450g/1lb
  fresh
salt and black pepper

1 Place the garlic, basil, hazelnuts, and cheese in a food processor or blender and process to a thick paste.

2 Cook the tagliatelle in lightly salted boiling water until just tender, then drain well.

3 Spoon the sauce into the hot pasta, tossing until melted. Sprinkle with pepper and serve hot.

--- COOK'S TIP ---

Italian ricotta cheese makes a good, though less low-fat, alternative to skimmed milk soft cheese in this recipe.

Spaghetti with Tuna Sauce

A speedy, and very tasty,w mid-week meal, which can also be made with other pasta shapes.

INGREDIENTS 🍎

Serves 4

225g/8oz dried spaghetti, or 450g/1lb
  fresh
1 garlic clove, crushed
400g/14oz can chopped tomatoes
425g/15oz can tuna in water, drained
  and flaked
2.5ml/½ tsp chilli sauce (optional)
4 pitted black olives, chopped
salt and black pepper

--- COOK'S TIP ---

If fresh tuna is available, use 450g/1lb, cut into small chunks, and add after step 2. Simmer for 6–8 minutes, then add the chilli sauce, olives, and pasta.

1 Cook the spaghetti in lightly salted boiling water for 12 minutes or until just tender. Drain well and keep hot.

2 Add the garlic and tomatoes to the saucepan and bring to a boil. Simmer, uncovered, for 2–3 minutes.

3 Add the tuna, chilli sauce, if using, olives, and spaghetti. Heat well, add the seasoning, and serve hot.

--- VARIATION ---

To make a less hot, herby version of this dish, omit the chilli sauce and add 60ml/ 4 tbsp chopped mixed fresh herbs instead.

MID-WEEK SUPPERS

When you are cooking for a family, week-day meals need to be filling fare. Recipes that are a complete main course in one dish, such as Minced Beef with Garlic Potatoes, or Mushroom and Bacon Risotto, are ideal. If you haven't much time on the day for cooking, there are quick recipes here that will appeal to children and adults alike: try Bacon Koftas, Greek Lamb Pie, or make a warming pot of Sausages and Beans with Dumplings.

Rich Beef Casserole

INGREDIENTS

Serves 4–6

1kg/2lb chuck steak, cut into cubes
2 onions, roughly chopped
1 bouquet garni
6 black peppercorns
15ml/1 tbsp red wine vinegar
1 bottle full-bodied red wine
45–60ml/3–4 tbsp olive oil
3 celery sticks, thickly sliced
50g/2oz/½ cup plain flour
300ml/½ pint/1¼ cups beef stock
30ml/2 tbsp tomato purée
2 garlic cloves, crushed
175g/6oz chestnut mushrooms,
   halved
400g/14oz can artichoke hearts,
   drained and halved
chopped fresh parsley and thyme,
   to garnish
creamy mashed potatoes, to serve

1 Place the meat in a bowl. Add the onions, bouquet garni, peppercorns, vinegar and wine. Stir well, cover and leave to marinate overnight.

2 The next day, preheat the oven to 160°C/325°F/Gas 3. Strain the meat, reserving the marinade. Pat the meat dry with kitchen paper.

3 Heat the oil in a large flameproof casserole and fry the meat and onions in batches, adding a little more oil, if necessary. Remove and set aside.

4 Add the celery to the casserole and fry until lightly browned. Remove and set aside with the meat and onions.

5 Sprinkle the flour into the casserole and cook for 1 minute. Gradually add the reserved marinade and the stock, and bring to the boil, stirring. Return the meat, onions and celery to the casserole, then stir in the tomato purée and crushed garlic.

6 Cover the casserole and cook in the oven for about 2¼ hours. Stir in the mushrooms and artichokes, cover again and cook for a further 15 minutes, until the meat is tender. Garnish with chopped parsley and thyme, and serve hot with creamy mashed potatoes.

Liver and Onions

Calves' liver is wonderfully tender and makes this simple dish mouthwateringly delicious. However it is expensive so substitute thinly sliced lamb's liver, if you prefer and cook over a low heat until just tender.

INGREDIENTS

Serves 4
60ml/4 tbsp oil
3 large onions, total weight about 600g/1lb6oz, sliced
450g/1lb calves' liver, cut into 5mm/ ¼in thick slices
salt and pepper
sage leaves, to garnish

1 Heat 45ml/3 tbsp of the oil in a large, heavy frying pan. Add the onions and a little seasoning, cover and cook over a low heat, stirring occasionally, for 25–30 minutes, until the onions are soft.

2 Uncover the pan, increase the heat to medium-high and cook the onions, stirring, for 5–7 minutes until golden. Using a slotted spoon, transfer to a bowl, leaving the oil in the pan.

3 Add the remaining oil to the pan and increase the heat to high. Working in batches so the liver is in a single layer, cook for 45–60 seconds a side until just browned on the outside, and pink inside and tender. Season, then transfer to a warm plate and keep warm while frying the remaining liver in the same way.

4 Return all the liver and the onions to the pan and cook over a high heat for 30–60 seconds. Serve at once, garnished with sage.

— COOK'S TIP —

The onions need to be covered during their initial cooking, if your frying pan does not have a lid, use foil as a cover.

Lamb Steaks with Mint Dressing

INGREDIENTS

Serves 4

4 shoulder steaks of lamb
1 large garlic clove, crushed
2.5cm/½in piece of root ginger, grated
10–12 coriander seeds, crushed
150ml/¼ pint/⅔ cup natural yogurt
30ml/2 tbsp olive oil
5ml/1 tsp walnut or sesame oil
15ml/1 tbsp orange juice
30ml/2 tbsp chopped fresh mint
½ green pepper, seeded and finely
   shredded
1 small red skinned onion, thinly sliced
½ oak leaf lettuce, torn into small
   pieces
salt and black pepper

1 Place the steaks on a flat dish or
tray. Pound together, or crush, the garlic, ginger and coriander seeds, then mix in half the yogurt and seasoning. Spread over the meat and leave for 1–2 hours, turning once.

2 Remove the steaks and scrape off
the marinade. Wipe the steaks dry and then brush with a little olive oil and sprinkle with seasoning. Grill or barbecue until as pink, or as well cooked as you wish.

3 Whisk the remaining olive oil and
the walnut or sesame oil into the remaining yogurt with the orange juice, mint, and seasoning to taste. Add a little water if it is too thick for your liking. Toss the pepper, onion and lettuce together lightly.

4 Serve the grilled steaks at once
with the tossed salad and the yogurt and mint dressing.

COOK'S TIP

Lamb shoulder steaks are the best value for this dish, but not always available – you could use leg steaks or chops instead.

Sausages and Beans with Dumplings

Sausages needn't be totally banned on a low fat diet, but choose them carefully. If you are unable to find a reduced-fat variety, choose turkey sausages instead, and always drain off any fat during cooking.

INGREDIENTS 🍎

Serves 4

450g/1lb half-fat sausages
1 medium onion, thinly sliced
1 green pepper, seeded and diced
1 small red chilli, sliced, or ½ tsp chilli sauce
400g/14oz can chopped tomatoes
250ml/8fl oz/1 cup beef stock
425g/15oz can red kidney beans, drained
salt and black pepper

For the dumplings

275g/10oz/2½ cups plain flour
10ml/2 tsp baking powder
225g/8oz/1 cup cottage cheese

1 Cook the sausages without fat in a non-stick pan until brown. Add the onion and pepper. Stir in the chilli, tomatoes, and stock; bring to the boil.

─── COOK'S TIP ───

To make a speedy, spicy (though not low fat) version of this recipe, use chorizo sausages or kabanos in place of the half-fat sausages. Cut in thick slices and add to the sauce in step 2.

2 Cover and simmer gently for 15–20 minutes, then add the beans and bring to the boil.

3 To make the dumplings, sift the flour and baking powder together and add enough water to mix to a firm dough. Roll out thinly and stamp out 16–18 rounds using a 7.5cm/3in cutter.

4 Place a small spoonful of cottage cheese on each round and bring the edges of the dough together, pinching to enclose. Arrange the dumplings over the sausages in the pan, cover the pan, and simmer for 10–12 minutes, until the dumplings are puffed. Serve hot.

Ragoût of Veal

If you are looking for a low calorie dish to treat yourself – or some guests – then this is perfect, and quick, too.

INGREDIENTS

Serves 4

450g/1lb veal fillet or loin
30ml/2 tbsp olive oil
10–12 tiny onions, kept whole
1 yellow pepper, seeded and cut in eight
1 orange or red pepper, seeded and cut in eight
3 plum tomatoes, peeled and quartered
4 sprigs of fresh basil
30ml/2 tbsp dry martini or sherry
salt and black pepper

1 Trim off any fat and cut the veal into cubes. Heat the oil in a frying pan and gently stir-fry the veal and onions until browned.

2 After a couple of minutes add the peppers and tomatoes. Continue stir-frying for another 4–5 minutes.

3 Add half the basil leaves, roughly chopped (keep some for garnish), the martini or sherry, and seasoning. Cook, stirring frequently, for another 10 minutes, or until the meat is tender.

4 Sprinkle with the remaining basil leaves and serve hot.

Lamb's Liver with Peppers

If you really want to push the boat out for a special occasion, then use sliced calves' liver instead of the lamb's.

INGREDIENTS

Serves 4

30ml/2 tbsp olive oil
2 shallots, sliced
450g/1lb lamb's liver, cut in thin strips
1 garlic clove, crushed
10ml/2 tsp green peppercorns, crushed (or more to taste)
½ red pepper, seeded and cut in strips
½ orange or yellow pepper, seeded and cut in strips
30ml/2 tbsp crème fraîche
salt and black pepper
rice or noodles, to serve

1 Heat the oil and fry the shallots briskly for 1 minute. Add the liver, garlic, peppercorns and peppers, then stir-fry for 3–4 minutes, or until no pink runs from the liver.

2 Stir in the crème fraîche, season to taste and serve immediately with noodles or rice.

COOK'S TIP

Lamb's liver is best when still very slightly pink in the middle, although many prefer it well cooked. With this recipe you could please everyone, but do watch closely as it soon overcooks.

Mushroom and Bacon Risotto

INGREDIENTS

Serves 4

30ml/2 tbsp sunflower oil
1 large onion, chopped
75g/3oz smoked bacon, chopped
325g/12oz Arborio or risotto rice
1–2 garlic cloves, crushed
15g/½oz dried sliced mushrooms,
  soaked in a little boiling water
175g/6oz mixed fresh mushrooms
1.2 litres/2 pints/5 cups hot stock
few sprigs of oregano or thyme
15g/½oz/1 tbsp butter
little dry white wine
45ml/3 tbsp peeled, chopped tomato
8–10 black olives, stoned and quartered
salt and black pepper
sprigs of thyme, to garnish

1 Heat the oil in a large, heavy-based pan with a lid. Gently cook the onion and bacon until the onion is tender and the bacon fat has run out.

2 Stir in the rice and garlic and cook over a high heat for 2–3 minutes, until the rice is well coated. Add the dried mushrooms and their liquid, the fresh mushrooms and half the stock, the oregano and seasoning. Bring gently to the boil, then reduce the heat to minimum. Cover tightly and leave to cook.

3 Check the liquid in the risotto occasionally by very gently stirring. If quite dry, slowly add more liquid. (Don't stir too often, as this lets the steam and flavour out.) Add more liquid as required until the rice is cooked, but not mushy.

4 Just before serving, stir in the butter, white wine, tomatoes and olives and check the seasoning. Serve hot, garnished with thyme sprigs.

Minced Beef Pie with Garlic Potatoes

This is almost a complete meal in itself, but you could add lots more vegetables to the meat to make it go further.

INGREDIENTS

Serves 4
450g/1lb lean minced beef
1 onion, chopped
3 carrots, sliced
4 tomatoes, peeled and chopped
300ml/½ pint/1¼ cups beef stock
5ml/1 tsp cornflour
15ml/1 tbsp chopped, mixed herbs, or 5ml/1 tsp dried
30ml/2 tbsp olive oil
2 garlic cloves, crushed
500g/1¼lb potatoes (3 large), par-cooked and sliced
salt and black pepper

1 Preheat the oven to 180°C/350°F/ Gas 4. Stir-fry the meat and onions in a large pan until browned. Add the carrots and tomatoes to the pan.

2 Stir in the stock, with the cornflour blended in, and the herbs. Bring to the boil and simmer for 2–3 minutes, then season to taste. Transfer to a shallow ovenproof dish.

3 Mix the oil, garlic and seasoning together. Layer the potatoes on top of the meat mixture, brushing liberally with the garlic oil. Cook for 30–40 minutes, until the potatoes are tender and golden. Serve with a green salad and crisp green beans or mange-tout.

COOK'S TIP

Leave the potatoes unpeeled, if you prefer, in this recipe, and incorporate other par-cooked root vegetables such as carrot, celeriac, swede or turnip, and layer them with the potatoes.

Greek Lamb Pie

INGREDIENTS 🍎

Serves 4

sunflower oil, for brushing
450g/1lb lean minced lamb
1 medium onion, sliced
1 garlic clove, crushed
400g/14oz can plum tomatoes
30ml/2 tbsp chopped fresh mint
5ml/1 tsp grated nutmeg
350g/12oz young spinach leaves
270g/10oz packet filo pastry
5ml/1 tsp sesame seeds
salt and black pepper

1 Preheat the oven to 200°C/400°F/ Gas 6. Lightly oil a 22cm/8½in round spring-form tin.

2 Cook the lamb and onion without fat in a non-stick pan until golden. Add the garlic, tomatoes, mint, nutmeg, and seasoning. Bring to a boil, stirring. Simmer, stirring occasionally, until most of the liquid has evaporated.

3 Wash the spinach and remove any tough stalks, then cook in only the water clinging to the leaves for about 2 minutes, until wilted.

4 Lightly brush each sheet of filo pastry with oil and lay in overlapping layers in the tin, leaving enough overhanging to wrap over the top.

5 Spoon in the meat and spinach, then wrap the pastry over to enclose, scrunching it slightly. Sprinkle with sesame seeds and bake for about 25–30 minutes, or until golden and crisp. Serve hot, with salad or vegetables.

COOK'S TIP

Choose filo pastry with large sheets, if possible. If yours aren't large enough to line the spring-form tin, arrange the smaller sheets two at a time in the tin, overlapping them slightly.

Pork Roast in a Blanket

INGREDIENTS 🍎

Serves 4

1.5kg/3lb lean pork loin joint
1 eating apple, cored and grated
40g/1½oz/¾ cup fresh breadcrumbs
30ml/2 tbsp chopped hazelnuts
15ml/1 tbsp Dijon mustard
15ml/1 tbsp snipped fresh chives
salt and black pepper

1 If necessary, trim the roast, leaving only a thin layer of fat.

2 Preheat the oven to 220°C/425°F/ Gas 7. Place the meat on a rack in a roasting tin, cover the meat with foil, and roast for 1 hour, then reduce the oven temperature to 180°C/350°F/Gas 4.

3 In a bowl, mix together the apple, breadcrumbs, nuts, mustard, chives, and seasoning. Remove the foil and spread the bread crumb mixture over the fat surface of the meat.

4 Roast the pork for 45–60 minutes, or until the juices run clear. Serve in slices with gravy.

VARIATION

For a change, use chopped almonds in place of the hazelnuts and substitute chopped fresh parsley for the chives.

Turkish Lamb and Apricot Stew

INGREDIENTS

Serves 4

1 large aubergine, cubed
30ml/2 tbsp sunflower oil
1 onion, chopped
1 garlic clove, crushed
5ml/1 tsp ground cinnamon
3 whole cloves
450g/1lb boned leg of lamb, cubed
400g/14oz can chopped tomatoes
115g/4oz/⅔ cup ready-to-eat dried
    apricots
115g/4oz canned chick-peas, drained
5ml/1 tsp clear honey
salt and black pepper
couscous, to serve
30ml/2 tbsp olive oil
30ml/2 tbsp chopped almonds, fried in
    a little oil
chopped fresh parsley

1 Place the aubergine in a colander, sprinkle with salt and leave for 30 minutes. Heat the oil in a flameproof casserole, add the onions and garlic and fry for 5 minutes, until softened.

2 Stir in the ground cinnamon and cloves and fry for 1 minute. Add the lamb and cook for 5–6 minutes, stirring occasionally until well browned.

3 Rinse, drain and pat dry the aubergine, add to the pan and cook for 3 minutes, stirring well. Add the tomatoes, 300ml/½ pint/1¼ cups water, apricots and seasoning. Bring to the boil, then cover and simmer gently for about 45 minutes.

4 Stir in the chick-peas and honey and cook for a further 15–20 minutes, or until the lamb is tender. Serve the stew acompanied by couscous with the olive oil, fried almonds and chopped parsley stirred in.

Country Pork with Parsley Cobbler

This hearty casserole is a
complete main course in one pot.

INGREDIENTS

Serves 4

450g/1lb boneless pork shoulder, diced
1 small swede, diced
2 carrots, sliced
2 parsnips, sliced
2 leeks, sliced
2 celery stalks, sliced
750ml/1¼ pints/3⅔ cups boiling beef
  stock
30ml/2 tbsp tomato purée
30ml/2 tbsp chopped fresh parsley
50g/2oz/¼ cup pearl barley
celery salt and black pepper

For the topping

150g/5oz/1 cup plain flour
5ml/1 tsp baking powder
90ml/6 tbsp low fat fromage frais
45ml/3 tbsp chopped fresh parsley

1 Preheat the oven to 180°C/350°F/
Gas 4. Cook the pork without fat, in
a non-stick pan until lightly browned.

2 Add the vegetables to the pan and
stir over medium heat until lightly
colored. Tip into a large casserole dish,
then stir in the stock, tomato purée,
parsley, and pearl barley.

3 Season with celery salt and pepper,
then cover and place in the oven
for about 1–1¼ hours, until the pork
and vegetables are tender.

4 For the topping, sift the flour and
baking powder with seasoning, then
stir in the fromage frais and parsley with
enough cold water to mix to a soft
dough. Roll out to about 1cm/½in
thickness and cut into 12–16 triangles.

5 Remove the casserole from the
oven and raise the temperature to
220°C/425°F/Gas 7.

6 Arrange the triangles over the
casserole, overlapping. Bake for
15–20 minutes, until puffed and golden.

--- COOK'S TIP ---

When mixing the cobbler topping, add
the water a little at a time, the dough
should be soft, but not sticky. If it is slightly too damp, dust the work surface with a
little flour before rolling out.

Pan-fried Mediterranean Lamb

The warm summery flavours of the Mediterranean are combined for a simple weekday meal.

INGREDIENTS

Serves 4
8 lean lamb cutlets
1 medium onion, thinly sliced
2 red peppers, seeded and sliced
400g/14oz can plum tomatoes
1 garlic clove, crushed
45ml/3 tbsp chopped fresh basil leaves
30ml/2 tbsp chopped black olives
salt and black pepper

1 Trim any excess fat from the lamb, then cook without fat in a non-stick pan until golden brown.

2 Add the onion and peppers to the pan. Cook, stirring, for a few minutes to soften, then add the plum tomatoes, garlic, and basil.

3 Cover and simmer for 20 minutes or until the lamb is tender. Stir in the olives, season, and serve hot with pasta.

VARIATION

This recipe would be equally good with skinless chicken breast fillets instead of the lamb cutlets.

Bacon Koftas

These easy koftas are good for outdoor summer barbecues, served with lots of salad.

INGREDIENTS

Serves 4
225g/8oz lean bacon, coarsely
  chopped
75g/3oz/1 cup fresh wholemeal
  breadcrumbs
2 spring onions, chopped
15ml/1 tbsp chopped fresh parsley
finely grated rind of 1 lemon
1 egg white
black pepper
paprika
lemon rind and fresh parsley leaves,
  to garnish

1 Place the bacon in a food processor together with the breadcrumbs, spring onions, parsley, lemon rind, egg white, and pepper. Process the mixture until it is finely chopped and begins to bind together.

2 Divide the bacon mixture into eight even-sized pieces and shape into long ovals around eight wooden or bamboo skewers.

3 Sprinkle the koftas with paprika and cook under a hot grill or on a barbecue for about 8–10 minutes, turning occasionally, until browned and cooked through. Garnish with lemon rind and parsley leaves, then serve hot with lemon rice and salad.

COOK'S TIP

Don't over-process the kofta mixture – it should be only just mixed. If you don't have a food processor, either mince the bacon, or chop it very finely by hand, then mix in the rest of the ingredients.

Louisiana Rice

INGREDIENTS

Serves 4

60ml/4 tbsp vegetable oil
1 small aubergine, diced
225g/8oz minced pork
1 green pepper, seeded and chopped
2 sticks celery, chopped
1 onion, chopped
1 garlic clove, crushed
5ml/1 tsp cayenne pepper
5ml/1 tsp paprika
5ml/1 tsp black pepper
2.5ml/½ tsp salt
5ml/1 tsp dried thyme
2.5ml/½ tsp dried oregano
475ml/16fl oz/2 cups chicken stock
225g/8oz chicken livers, minced
150g/5oz/¾ cup long grain rice
1 bay leaf
45ml/3 tbsp chopped fresh parsley
celery leaves, to garnish

1 Heat the oil in a frying pan until really hot, then add the aubergine and stir-fry for about 5 minutes.

2 Add the pork and cook for about 6–8 minutes, until browned, using a wooden spoon to break any lumps.

3 Add the pepper, celery, onion, garlic and all the spices and herbs. Cover and cook on a high heat for 5–6 minutes, stirring frequently from the bottom to scrape up and distribute the crispy brown bits.

4 Pour on the chicken stock and stir to clean the bottom of the pan. Cover and cook for 6 minutes over a moderate heat. Stir in the chicken livers, cook for 2 minutes, then stir in the rice and add the bay leaf.

5 Reduce the heat, cover and simmer for about 6–7 minutes. Turn off the heat and leave to stand for a further 10–15 minutes until the rice is tender. Remove the bay leaf and stir in the chopped parsley. Serve the rice hot, garnished with the celery leaves.

Moroccan Chicken Couscous

INGREDIENTS

Serves 4

15ml/1 tbsp butter
15ml/1 tbsp sunflower oil
4 chicken portions
2 onions, finely chopped
2 garlic cloves, crushed
2.5ml/½ tsp ground cinnamon
1.25ml/¼ tsp ground ginger
1.25ml/¼ tsp ground turmeric
30ml/2 tbsp orange juice
10ml/2 tsp clear honey
salt and black pepper
fresh mint sprigs, to garnish

For the couscous

350g/12oz/2¼ cups couscous
5ml/1 tsp salt
10ml/2 tsp caster sugar
30ml/2 tbsp sunflower oil
2.5ml/½ tsp ground cinnamon
pinch of grated nutmeg
15ml/1 tbsp orange blossom water
30ml/2 tbsp sultanas
50g/2oz/½ cup chopped blanched
  almonds
45ml/3 tbsp chopped pistachio nuts

1 Heat the butter and oil in a large pan and add the chicken portions, skin side down. Fry for 3–4 minutes, until the skin is golden, then turn over.

2 Add the onions, garlic, spices and a pinch of salt and pour over the orange juice and 300ml/½ pint/1¼ cups of water. Cover and bring to the boil, then reduce the heat and simmer for about 30 minutes.

3 Meanwhile, place the couscous and salt in a bowl and cover with 350ml/12fl oz/1½ cups water. Stir once and leave to stand for 5 minutes. Add the caster sugar, 15ml/1 tbsp of the oil, the cinnamon, nutmeg, orange blossom water and sultanas to the couscous and mix very well.

4 Heat the remaining 15ml/1 tbsp of the oil in a pan and lightly fry the almonds until golden. Stir into the couscous with the pistachio nuts.

5 Line a steamer with greaseproof paper and spoon in the couscous. Sit the steamer over the chicken (or over a pan of boiling water) and steam for 10 minutes.

6 Remove the steamer and keep covered. Stir the honey into the chicken liquid and boil rapidly for 3–4 minutes. Spoon the couscous on to a warmed serving platter and top with the chicken, with a little of the sauce spooned over. Garnish with fresh mint and serve with the remaining sauce.

Spiced Lamb with Apricots

INGREDIENTS

Serves 4

115g/4oz/½ cup ready-to-eat dried
  apricots
50g/2oz/⅓ cup seedless raisins
2.5ml/½ tsp saffron strands
150ml/¼ pint/⅔ cup orange juice
15ml/1 tbsp red wine vinegar
30–45ml/2–3 tbsp olive oil
1.5 kg/3lb leg of lamb, boned
  and cubed
1 onion, chopped
2 garlic cloves, crushed
10ml/2 tsp ground cumin
1.25ml/¼ tsp ground cloves
15ml/1 tbsp ground coriander
30ml/2 tbsp plain flour
600ml/1 pint/2½ cups lamb stock
45ml/3 tbsp chopped fresh coriander
salt and black pepper
saffron rice mixed with toasted
  almonds and chopped fresh
  coriander, to serve

1 Mix together the dried apricots, raisins, saffron, orange juice and vinegar in a bowl. Cover and leave to soak for 2–3 hours.

2 Preheat the oven to 160°C/325°F/ Gas 3. Heat 30ml/2 tbsp oil in a large flameproof casserole and brown the lamb in batches. Remove and set aside. Add the onion and garlic with a little more of the remaining oil, if necessary, and cook until softened.

3 Stir in the spices and flour and cook for a further 1–2 minutes. Return the meat to the casserole. Stir in the stock, fresh coriander and the soaked fruit with its liquid. Add seasoning, then bring to the boil.

4 Cover the casserole and cook for 1½ hours (adding a little extra stock if necessary), or until the lamb is tender. Serve with saffron rice mixed with toasted almonds and fresh coriander.

Sausage and Bean Ragoût

An economical and nutritious main course that children will love. Garlic and herb bread makes an ideal accompaniment.

INGREDIENTS

Serves 4

350g/12oz/2 cups dried flageolet
  beans, soaked overnight
45ml/3 tbsp olive oil
1 onion, finely chopped
2 garlic cloves, crushed
450g/1lb good-quality chunky
  sausages, skinned and thickly sliced
15ml/1 tbsp tomato purée
30ml/2 tbsp fresh chopped parsley
15ml/1 tbsp fresh chopped thyme
400g/14oz can chopped tomatoes
salt and black pepper
chopped fresh thyme and parsley,
to garnish

1 Drain and rinse the soaked beans and place them in a pan with enough water to cover. Bring to the boil, cover the pan and simmer for about 1 hour, or until tender. Drain the beans and set aside.

2 Heat the oil and fry the onion, garlic and sausages until golden.

3 Stir in the tomato purée, chopped parsley and thyme, tomatoes and seasoning, then bring to the boil.

4 Add the beans, then cover and cook gently for about 15 minutes, stirring occasionally, until the sausages are cooked through. Garnish with extra chopped fresh herbs and serve.

Lamb Pie with a Potato Crust

A pleasant change from meat and potatoes – healthier, too.

INGREDIENTS

Serves 4
750g/1½lb potatoes, diced
30ml/2 tbsp skimmed milk
15ml/1 tbsp wholegrain or French
   mustard
450g/1lb lean minced lamb
1 onion, chopped
2 celery stalks, sliced
2 carrots, diced
150ml/¼ pint/⅔ cup beef stock
60ml/4 tbsp rolled oats
15ml/1 tbsp Worcestershire sauce
30ml/2 tbsp fresh chopped rosemary,
   or 10ml/2 tsp dried
salt and black pepper

1 Cook the potatoes in boiling, lightly salted water until tender. Drain and mash until smooth, then stir in the milk and mustard. Meanwhile, preheat the oven to 200°C/400°F/Gas 6.

2 Break up the lamb with a fork and cook without fat in a non-stick pan until lightly browned. Add the onion, celery, and carrots to the pan and cook for 2–3 minutes, stirring.

3 Stir in the stock and rolled oats. Bring to the boil, then add the Worcestershire sauce and rosemary, and season to taste with salt and pepper.

4 Turn the meat mixture into a 1.8 litre/3 pint/7 cup ovenproof dish and spread over the potato topping evenly, swirling with the edge of a knife. Bake for 30–35 minutes, or until golden. Serve hot with fresh vegetables.

— COOK'S TIP —

You can prepare this pie up to a day ahead. Cover and chill until ready to bake. Allow the pie to come back to room temperature before baking, or add a few minutes extra cooking time.

Baked Pasta Bolognese

INGREDIENTS

Serves 4

30ml/2 tbsp olive oil
1 onion, chopped
1 garlic clove, crushed
1 carrot, diced
2 celery sticks, chopped
2 rashers streaky bacon, finely chopped
5 button mushrooms, chopped
450g/1lb lean minced beef
120ml/4fl oz/½ cup red wine
15ml/1 tbsp tomato purée
200g/7oz can chopped tomatoes
sprig of fresh thyme
225g/8oz/2 cups dried penne pasta
300ml/½ pint/1¼ cups milk
25g/1oz/2 tbsp butter
25g/1oz/2 tbsp plain flour
150g/5oz/1 cup cubed mozzarella
   cheese
60ml/4 tbsp grated Parmesan cheese
salt and black pepper
fresh basil sprigs, to garnish

1 Heat the oil in a pan and fry the onion, garlic, carrot and celery for 6 minutes, until the onions have softened.

2 Add the bacon and continue frying for 3–4 minutes. Stir in the mushrooms, fry for 2 minutes, then add the beef. Fry on a high heat until well browned all over.

3 Pour in the red wine, the tomato purée dissolved in 45ml/3 tbsp water, and the tomatoes, then add the thyme and season well. Bring to the boil, cover the pan and simmer gently for about 30 minutes.

4 Preheat the oven to 200°C/400°F/ Gas 6. Bring a pan of water to the boil, add a little oil and cook the pasta for 10 minutes.

5 Meanwhile, place the milk, butter and flour in a saucepan, heat gently and whisk continuously with a balloon whisk until thickened. Stir in the mozzarella cheese, 30ml/2 tbsp of the Parmesan and season lightly.

6 Drain the pasta when it is ready and stir into the cheese sauce. Uncover the Bolognese sauce and boil rapidly for 2 minutes to reduce the liquid.

7 Spoon the sauce into an ovenproof dish, top with the pasta mixture and sprinkle the remaining 30ml/2 tbsp Parmesan cheese evenly over the top. Bake for 25 minutes until golden. Garnish with basil and serve hot.

Curried Lamb and Lentils

This colourful curry is packed with protein and is low in fat, too.

INGREDIENTS 🍎

Serves 4

8 lean, boneless lamb leg steaks, about
   500g/1¼lb total weight
1 medium onion, chopped
2 medium carrots, diced
1 celery stalk, chopped
15ml/1 tbsp hot curry paste
30ml/2 tbsp tomato purée
475ml/16fl oz/2 cups stock
175g/6oz/1 cup green lentils
salt and black pepper
fresh coriander leaves, to garnish
boiled rice, to serve

1 In a large, non-stick pan, cook the lamb steaks without fat until browned, turning once.

2 Add the vegetables and cook for 2 minutes, then stir in the curry paste, tomato purée, stock and lentils.

3 Bring to the boil, cover, and simmer gently for 30 minutes until tender. Add more stock, if necessary. Season and serve with coriander and rice.

—— Cook's Tip ——

Use fresh lamb stock if you can for this curry, however a chicken or vegetable stock cube, dissolved in boiling water will work just as well.

Golden Pork and Apricot Casserole

The rich golden color and warm spicy flavor of this simple casserole make it ideal for chilly winter days.

INGREDIENTS 🍎

Serves 4

4 lean pork loin chops
1 medium onion, thinly sliced
2 yellow peppers, seeded and
   sliced
10ml/2 tsp medium hot curry powder
15ml/1 tbsp plain flour
250ml/8fl oz/1 cup chicken stock
115g/4oz/⅔ cup dried apricots
30ml/2 tbsp wholegrain mustard
salt and black pepper

1 Trim the excess fat from the pork and cook without fat in a large, heavy or non-stick pan until lightly browned.

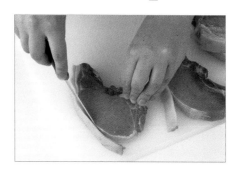

2 Add the onion and peppers to the pan and stir over a moderate heat for 5 minutes. Stir in the curry powder and the flour.

3 Add the stock, stirring, then add the apricots and mustard. Cover and simmer for 25–30 minutes, until tender. Adjust the seasoning and serve hot, with rice or new potatoes.

—— Variation ——

To make Golden Lamb and Apricot Casserole, substitute lamb leg chops or steaks for the pork chops.

ROASTS, PIES & HOT-POTS

Slow-cooked, traditional recipes are everyone's favourite, and
here you'll find time-honoured classics, such as Braised Brisket
with Dumplings, and Steak, Kidney and Mushroom Pie that
are perfect for family meals, alongside less well known, but just
as tasty, dishes like Butterflied Cumin and Garlic Lamb, and
Pork Chops with Plums. There are also delicious twists on old-
fashioned roasts, stews and casseroles to try, such as Beef
Paprika with Roasted Peppers, or Herby Lamb Hot-pot – both
are ideal for informal entertaining at the weekend.

Beef Paprika with Roasted Peppers

This dish is perfect for family suppers – roasting the peppers gives a new dimension.

INGREDIENTS

Serves 4
30ml/2 tbsp olive oil
675g/1½lb chuck steak, cut into
4cm/1½in cubes
2 onions, chopped
1 garlic clove, crushed
15ml/1 tbsp plain flour
15ml/1 tbsp paprika, plus extra
to garnish
400g/14oz can chopped tomatoes
2 red peppers, halved and seeded
150ml/¼ pint/⅔ cup crème fraîche
salt and black pepper
buttered noodles, to serve

1 Preheat the oven to 140°C/275°F/ Gas 1. Heat the oil in a large flameproof casserole and brown the meat in batches. Remove the meat from the casserole using a slotted spoon.

2 Add the onions and garlic and fry gently until softened. Stir in the flour and paprika and continue cooking for a further 1–2 minutes, stirring.

3 Return the meat and any juices that have collected on the plate to the casserole, then add the chopped tomatoes and seasoning. Bring to the boil, stirring, then cover and cook in the oven for 2½ hours.

4 Meanwhile, place the peppers skin-side up on a grill rack and grill until the skins have blistered and charred. Cool, then peel off the skins. Cut the flesh into strips. Add to the casserole and cook for a further 15–30 minutes, or until the meat is tender.

5 Stir in the crème fraîche and sprinkle with a little paprika. Serve hot with buttered noodles.

COOK'S TIP

Take care when browning the meat and add only a few pieces at a time. If you overcrowd the pan, steam is created and the meat will never brown!

Beef Olives

INGREDIENTS

Serves 4

25g/1oz/2 tbsp butter
2 slices bacon, finely chopped
115g/4oz mushrooms, chopped
15ml/1 tbsp chopped fresh parsley
grated rind and juice of 1 lemon
115g/4oz/2 cups fresh breadcrumbs
675g/1½lb topside of beef, cut into 8
  thin slices
45ml/3 tbsp plain flour
45ml/3 tbsp oil
2 onions, sliced
450ml/¾ pint/2 cups beef stock
salt and pepper
chopped fresh parsley, to garnish

1 Preheat the oven to 160°C/325°F/ Gas 3. Heat the butter, add the bacon and mushrooms and fry for about 3 minutes, then mix them with the parsley, lemon rind and juice, breadcrumbs and seasoning.

2 Spread an equal amount of the breadcrumb mixture evenly over the beef slices, leaving a narrow border clear around the edge.

3 Roll up the slices and tie securely with fine string, then dip the beef rolls in the flour to coat lightly.

4 Heat the oil in a heavy shallow pan, then fry the beef rolls until lightly browned. Remove the beef rolls from the pan and keep warm.

5 Add the onions to the pan and fry until browned. Stir in the remaining flour and cook until lightly browned. Pour in the stock, stirring constantly, then bring to the boil, stirring and simmer for 2–3 minutes.

6 Transfer the beef rolls to a casserole, pour over the sauce, then cover the casserole tightly and cook in the oven for 2 hours. Lift out the 'olives' using a slotted spoon and remove the string. Then return them to the sauce and serve hot, garnished with parsley.

--- COOK'S TIP ---

At the end of the cooking the onions can be puréed with a little of the stock, then stirred back into the casserole to make a smooth sauce, if you prefer.

Lamb, Leek and Apple Pie

INGREDIENTS

Serves 4

675g/1½lb lamb neck fillets, cut into
    12 pieces
115g/4oz gammon, diced
1 onion, thinly sliced
350g/12oz leeks, sliced
1 large cooking apple, peeled, cored
    and sliced
1.25–2.5ml/¼–½tsp ground allspice
1.25–2.5ml/¼–½tsp freshly grated
    nutmeg
150ml/¼ pint/⅔ cup lamb, beef or
    vegetable stock
225g/8oz ready-made shortcrust pastry
beaten egg or milk, to glaze
salt and black pepper

1 Preheat the oven to 200°C/400°F/
Gas 6. Layer the meats, onion, leeks
and apple in a 900ml/1½ pint/3¾ cup
pie dish, sprinkling in the spices and
seasoning as you go. Pour in the stock.

2 Roll out the pastry to 2cm/¾in
larger than the top of the pie dish.
Cut a narrow strip from around the
pastry, fit it around the dampened rim
of the dish, then brush with water.

3 Lay the pastry over the dish, and
press the edges together to seal
them. Brush the top with beaten egg
or milk, and make a hole in the centre.

4 Bake the pie for 20 minutes, then
reduce the oven temperature to
180°C/350°F/Gas 4 and continue to
bake for 1–1¼ hours, covering the pie
with foil if the pastry begins to become
too brown.

Beef Wellington

Beef Wellington is supposedly so-
named because of the resemblance of
its shape and rich brown colour to
the Duke of Wellington's boot.

INGREDIENTS

Serves 8

1.4kg/3lb fillet of beef
15g/½oz/1 tbsp butter
30ml/2 tbsp oil
½ small onion, finely chopped
175g/6oz mushrooms, chopped
175g/6oz liver pâté
lemon juice
few drops of Worcestershire sauce
400g/14oz ready-made puff pastry
salt and black pepper
beaten egg, to glaze

1 Preheat the oven to 220°C/425°F/
Gas 7. Season the beef with pepper, then tie it at intervals with string.

2 Heat the butter and oil in a roasting
tin. Brown the beef over a high
heat, then cook in the oven for 20
minutes. Cool and remove the string.

3 Scrape the cooking juices into a
pan, add the onion and mushrooms and cook until tender. Cool,
then mix with the pâté. Add lemon
juice and Worcestershire sauce.

4 Roll out the pastry to a large
5mm/¼in thick rectangle. Spread
the pâté mixture on the beef, then
place it in the centre of the pastry.
Damp the edges of the pastry, then
fold over to make a neat parcel, tuck-
ing in the ends neatly; press to seal.

5 Place the parcel on a baking sheet
with the join underneath and
brush with beaten egg. Bake for 25–45
minutes, depending how well done
you like the beef to be.

Oxtail Braised in Red Wine

Always plan to cook oxtail one or two days before you wish to eat it. This gives you time to skim off the fat before serving.

INGREDIENTS

Serves 3–4

60ml/4 tbsp sunflower oil
1 oxtail (about 1kg/2¼lb), cut in pieces
2 onions
2 carrots, quartered
2 celery sticks, cut in pieces
300ml/½ pint/1¼ cups beef stock
300ml/½ pint/1¼ cups red wine
bouquet garni
15g/½oz/1 tbsp plain flour
225g/8oz can chopped tomatoes
salt and black pepper
15ml/1 tbsp chopped fresh parsley, to garnish

1 Heat half the oil in a large flame-proof casserole or ovenproof pan with a tight-fitting lid. Sauté the pieces of oxtail until well browned.

2 Preheat the oven to 160°C/325°F/ Gas 3. Add one of the onions, sliced, the pieces of carrot and celery, the stock, wine, bouquet garni, and seasoning. Bring to the boil and then cook in the oven for 1 hour.

3 Baste and stir well, reduce the oven temperature to 150°C/300°F/Gas 2 for 1¼–2 hours, or until the meat is very tender. Remove from the oven.

4 Leave to cool completely, then discard the surface fat and reheat. Remove the oxtail and reserve. Strain the stock; discard the vegetables. Pre-heat the oven to 180°C/350°F/Gas 4.

5 Fry the remaining onion, sliced, with the remaining oil in a large pan until golden. Stir in the flour and cook, stirring, until turning golden.

6 Gradually stir in the stock, a little at a time as it thickens. Bring back to the boil and then stir in the toma-toes. Add the oxtail, and seasoning to taste. Cover and cook in the oven for 30 minutes, or until the oxtail is heated through and really tender. Serve hot, sprinkled with the fresh parsley.

Braised Brisket with Dumplings

Brisket is very underrated and most often eaten as salt beef or pastrami these days. Given plenty of gentle cooking it produces a deliciously tender pot roast for eating hot with dumplings, or to serve cold with baked potatoes and salad.

INGREDIENTS

Serves 6–8

15ml/1 tbsp sunflower oil
2 onions, sliced
900g/2lb piece of rolled brisket, tied
300ml/½ pint/1¼ cups hot beef stock
300ml/½ pint/1¼ cups beer
2 bay leaves
few parsley stalks
2 parsnips, chopped
2 carrots, sliced
½ swede, chopped

For the dumplings

25g/1oz/2 tbsp butter
175g/6oz/1¼ cups self-raising
   flour, sifted
5ml/1 tsp dry mustard powder
5ml/1 tsp each dried sage, thyme and
   parsley
salt and black pepper
fresh herb sprigs, such as parsley,
   oregano or thyme, to garnish

1 Preheat the oven to 160°C/325°F/ Gas 3. Heat the oil in a large flameproof casserole or ovenproof pan and fry the onions until well browned.

2 Place the meat on top, then add the hot stock, the beer, bay leaves and parsley stalks and bring to the boil. Cover and transfer to the oven for 2 hours, basting occasionally.

3 Meanwhile, prepare the vegetables and make the dumplings. Rub the butter into the flour, then mix in the mustard powder, herbs and seasoning, and add sufficient water to mix to a soft dough mixture. Shape into about 12 small balls.

4 When the meat is just about tender, add the vegetables and cook for 20 minutes. Check the seasoning, add the dumplings and continue cooking for 15 minutes, until swollen. Serve hot, garnished with herb sprigs.

Herby Lamb Hot-pot

Browning the lamb and kidneys, plus all the extra vegetables and herbs, add flavour to the traditional basic ingredients.

INGREDIENTS

Serves 4

40g/1½oz/3 tbsp dripping, or 45ml/ 3 tbsp oil
8 middle neck lamb chops, about 1kg/2lb total weight
175g/6oz lamb's kidneys, cut into large pieces
1kg/2lb potatoes, thinly sliced
3 carrots, thickly sliced
450g/1lb leeks, sliced
3 celery sticks, sliced
15ml/1 tbsp chopped fresh thyme
30ml/2 tbsp chopped fresh parsley
small sprig of rosemary
600ml/1 pint/2½ cups veal stock
salt and black pepper

1 Preheat the oven to 170°C/325°F/ Gas 3. Heat the dripping or oil in a frying pan and brown the chops and kidneys in batches, then reserve the fat.

2 In a large casserole, make alternate layers of lamb chops, kidneys, three-quarters of the potatoes and the carrots, leeks and celery, sprinkling the herbs and seasoning over each layer as you go. Tuck the rosemary sprig down the side.

3 Arrange the remaining potatoes on top. Pour over the stock, brush with the reserved fat, then cover and bake for 2½ hours. Increase the oven temperature to 220°C/425°F/Gas 7. Uncover and cook for 30 minutes.

Pork Chops with Plums

INGREDIENTS

Serves 4

450g/1lb ripe plums, halved and stoned
300ml/½ pint/1¼ cups apple juice
40g/1½oz/3 tbsp butter
15ml/1 tbsp oil
4 pork chops, about 200g/7oz each
1 onion, finely chopped
grated nutmeg
salt and black pepper
fresh sage leave, to garnish

1 Heat the butter and oil in a large frying pan and fry the chops until brown on both sides, then transfer them to a plate.

2 Meanwhile, simmer the plums in the apple juice until tender. Strain off and reserve the juice, then purée half the plums with a little of the juice.

3 Add the onion to the pan and cook gently until soft, but not coloured. Return the chops to the pan. Pour over the plum purée and all the juice.

4 Simmer, uncovered, for 10–15 minutes, until the chops are cooked through. Add the remaining plums to the pan, then add the nutmeg and seasoning. Warm the sauce through over a medium heat and serve garnished with fresh sage leaves.

--- COOK'S TIP ---

Use boneless pork steaks in place of the chops, if you like.

Roast Beef with Yorkshire Puddings

For this classic Sunday lunchtime meal, choose a joint of beef on the bone, such as sirloin or rib, or a boned and rolled joint of sirloin, rib or topside.

INGREDIENTS

Serves 6
1.75kg/4lb joint of beef
30–60ml/2–4 tbsp dripping or oil
300ml/½ pint/¼ cups vegetable or
  veal stock, wine or water
salt and pepper

For the Yorkshire puddings
50g/2oz/½ cup plain flour
1 egg, beaten
150ml/¼ pint/⅔ cup mixed water
  and milk
dripping or oil, for cooking

1 Weigh the beef and calculate the cooking time, allowing 15 minutes per 450g/1lb plus 15 minutes for rare meat, 20 minutes plus 20 minutes for medium and 25–30 minutes plus 25 minutes for well-done.

2 Preheat the oven to 220°C/425°F/ Gas 7. Heat the dripping or oil in a roasting tin in the oven.

3 Place the meat on a rack, fat-side uppermost, then place the rack in the roasting tin.

4 Baste the beef with the dripping or oil, and cook for the required time, basting occasionally.

5 To make the Yorkshire puddings, stir the flour, salt and pepper together in a bowl and form a well in the centre. Pour the egg into the well, then slowly pour in the milk, stirring in the flour to give a smooth batter. Leave to stand for 30 minutes.

6 A few minutes before the meat is ready, spoon a little dripping or oil in each of 12 patty tins and place in the oven until very hot. Remove the meat from the oven, season, then cover loosely with foil and keep warm.

7 Quickly divide the batter among the patty tins, then bake for 15–20 minutes, until well risen and brown.

8 Spoon off the fat from the roasting tin. Add the stock, wine or water, stirring to dislodge the sediment, and boil for a few minutes. Check the seasoning, then serve with the beef and Yorkshire puddings.

Irish Stew

INGREDIENTS
Serves 4

4 slices smoked streaky bacon,
  chopped
2 celery sticks, chopped
2 large onions, sliced
8 middle neck lamb chops, about
  1kg/2lb total weight
1kg/2lb potatoes, sliced
300ml/½ pint/1¼ cups brown veal
  stock or water
22.5ml/1½ tbsp Worcestershire sauce
5ml/1 tsp anchovy sauce
salt and black pepper
chopped fresh parsley, to garnish

1 Preheat the oven to 160°C/325°F/
Gas 3. Fry the bacon for about 3–5
minutes until the fat runs, then add the
celery and a third of the onions and
cook, stirring occasionally, until
browned.

2 Layer the lamb chops, potatoes,
vegetables and bacon and remaining onions in a heavy flameproof casserole, seasoning each layer, and finishing
with a layer of potatoes.

3 Stir the veal stock or water,
Worcestershire sauce and anchovy
sauce into the bacon and vegetable
cooking juices in the pan and bring to
the boil. Pour into the casserole,
adding water if necessary so the liquid
comes half way up the casserole.

4 Cover the casserole tightly, then
cook in the oven for 3 hours, until
the meat and vegetables are tender.
Serve hot, sprinkled with chopped
fresh parsley.

COOK'S TIP

The mutton that originally gave the
flavour to Irish Stew is often difficult to
obtain nowadays, so other flavourings are
added to compensate.

Butterflied Cumin and Garlic Lamb

Ground cumin and garlic give the lamb a wonderful Middle-Eastern flavour, although you may prefer a simple oil, lemon and herb marinade instead.

INGREDIENTS

Serves 6

1.75kg/4lb leg of lamb
60ml/4 tbsp olive oil
30ml/2 tbsp ground cumin
4–6 garlic cloves, crushed
salt and black pepper
toasted almond and raisin-studded
  pilaff, to serve
coriander sprigs and lemon wedges,
  to garnish

1 To butterfly the lamb, cut away the meat from the bone using a small sharp knife. Remove any excess fat and the thin, parchment-like membrane. Bat out the meat to an even thickness, then prick the fleshy side of the lamb well with the tip of a knife.

2 In a bowl, mix together the oil, cumin and garlic and season with pepper. Spoon the mixture all over the lamb, then rub it well into the crevices. Cover and leave to marinate overnight.

3 Preheat the oven to 200°C/400°F/ Gas 6. Spread the lamb, skin-side down, on a rack in a roasting tin. Season with salt and roast for 45–60 minutes, until crusty brown on the outside but still pink in the centre.

4 Remove the lamb from the oven and leave it to rest for about 10 minutes. Cut into diagonal slices and serve with the toasted almond and raisin-studded pilaff. Garnish with coriander sprigs and lemon wedges.

— COOK'S TIP —

The lamb may be barbecued rather than grilled. Thread it on to two long skewers and set it on the barbecue grid. Grill for 20–25 minutes on each side, until it is cooked to your liking.

Pot-roast Pork with Celery

INGREDIENTS

Serves 4

15ml/1 tbsp oil
50g/2oz/4 tbsp butter
about 1kg/2lb boned and rolled loin
  of pork, rind removed and well
  trimmed
1 onion, chopped
bouquet garni
3 sprigs fresh dill
150ml/¼ pint/⅔ cup medium-bodied
  dry white wine
150ml/¼ pint/⅔ cup water
sticks from 1 celery head, cut into
  2.5cm/1in lengths
30ml/2 tbsp plain flour
150ml/½ pint/⅔ cup double cream
squeeze of lemon juice
salt and black pepper
chopped fresh dill, to garnish

1 Heat the oil and half the butter in a heavy flameproof casserole just large enough to hold the pork and celery, then add the pork and brown evenly. Transfer the pork to a plate.

2 Add the onion to the casserole and cook until softened but not coloured. Place the bouquet garni and the dill sprigs on the onions, then place the pork on top and add any juices on the plate.

3 Pour the wine and water over the pork, season, cover tightly and simmer gently for 30 minutes.

4 Turn the pork, arrange the celery around it, then re-cover and continue to cook for about 40 minutes, until the pork and celery are tender.

5 Transfer the pork and celery to a warmed serving plate, cover and keep warm. Discard the bouquet garni and dill.

6 Mash the remaining butter with the flour, then whisk small pieces at a time into the cooking liquid while it is barely simmering. Cook for 2–3 minutes, stirring occasionally. Stir the cream into the casserole, bring to the boil and add a squeeze of lemon juice.

7 Slice the pork, pour some of the sauce over the slices and garnish with chopped dill. Serve the remaining sauce separately.

Beef in Guinness

INGREDIENTS

Serves 6

1kg/2lb chuck steak, cut into 4cm/
   1½in cubes
plain flour, for coating
45ml/3 tbsp oil
1 large onion, sliced
1 carrot, thinly sliced
2 celery sticks, thinly sliced
10ml/2 tsp sugar
5ml/1 tsp English mustard powder
15ml/1 tbsp tomato purée
2.5 x 7.5cm/1 x 3in strip orange rind
bouquet garni
600ml/1 pint/2½ cups Guinness
salt and black pepper

1 Toss the beef in flour to coat. Heat 30ml/2 tbsp oil in a large, shallow pan, then cook the beef in batches until lightly browned. Transfer to a bowl.

2 Add the remaining oil to the pan, then cook the onions until well browned, adding the carrot and celery towards the end.

3 Stir in the sugar, mustard, tomato purée, orange rind, Guinness and seasoning, then add the bouquet garni and bring to the boil. Return the meat, and any juices in the bowl, to the pan; add water, if necessary, so the meat is covered. Cover the pan tightly and cook gently for 2–2½ hours, until the meat is very tender.

Steak, Kidney and Mushroom Pie

INGREDIENTS

Serves 4

30ml/2 tbsp oil
1 onion, chopped
115g/4oz bacon, chopped
500g/1¼lb chuck steak, diced
30ml/2 tbsp plain flour
115g/4oz lamb's kidneys
400ml/14fl oz/1⅔ cups beef stock
large bouquet garni
115g/4oz button mushrooms
225g/8oz ready-made puff pastry
beaten egg, to glaze
salt and black pepper

1 Preheat the oven to 160°C/325°F/ Gas 3. Heat the oil in a heavy-based pan, then cook the bacon and onion until lightly browned.

2 Toss the steak in the flour. Stir the meat into the pan in batches and cook, stirring, until browned.

3 Toss the kidneys in flour and add to the pan with the bouquet garni. Transfer to a casserole dish, then pour in the stock, cover and cook in the oven for 2 hours. Stir in the mushrooms and seasoning and leave to cool.

4 Preheat the oven to 220°C/425°F/ Gas 7. Roll out the pastry to about 2cm/¾in larger than the top of a 1.2 litre/2 pint/5 cup pie dish. Cut off a narrow strip from the pastry and fit around the dampened rim of the dish. Brush the pastry strip with water.

5 Tip the meat mixture, into the dish. Lay the pastry over the dish, press the edges together to seal, then knock them up with the back of a knife.

6 Make a small slit in the pastry, brush with beaten egg and bake for 20 minutes. Lower the oven temperature to 180°C/350°F/Gas 4 and bake for a further 20 minutes, until the pastry is risen, golden and crisp.

Oatmeal and Herb Rack of Lamb

Ask the butcher to remove the chine bone for you (this is the long bone that runs along the eye of the meat) – this will make carving easier.

INGREDIENTS

Serves 6

2 best end necks of lamb, about
   1kg/2lb
finely grated rind of 1 lemon
60ml/4 tbsp medium oatmeal
50g/2oz/1 cup fresh white breadcrumbs
60ml/4 tbsp chopped fresh parsley
25g/1oz/2 tbsp butter, melted
30ml/2 tbsp clear honey
salt and black pepper
roasted baby vegetables and gravy,
   to serve
fresh herb sprigs, to garnish

1 Preheat the oven to 200°C/400°F/ Gas 6. Using a small sharp knife, cut through the skin and meat about 2.5cm/1in from the tips of the bones. Pull off the fatty meat to expose the bones, then scrape around each bone tip until completely clean.

2 Trim all the skin and most of the fat off the meat, then lightly score the fat. Repeat with the second rack.

3 Mix together the lemon rind, oatmeal, breadcrumbs, parsley and seasoning, then stir in the melted butter.

4 Brush the fatty side of each rack with honey, then press the oatmeal mixture evenly over the surface.

5 Place the racks in a large roasting tin with the oatmeal-coated sides uppermost. Roast for 40–50 minutes, depending on whether you like rare or medium-cooked lamb. Cover loosely with foil. To serve, slice each rack into three and accompany with roasted baby vegetables and gravy made with the pan juices. Garnish with fresh herb sprigs.

Glazed Ham with Spiced Peaches

One of the most pleasing things about today's joints of gammon or bacon is there is so little waste. They're easy to cook, too, and can be served hot or cold.

INGREDIENTS

Serves 6

1.5kg/3–3½lb joint of gammon or boiling bacon
600ml/1 pint/2½ cups cider
15ml/1 tbsp ground cinnamon
few black peppercorns, crushed
60–90ml/4–6 tbsp redcurrant jelly
425g/15oz can peach slices in fruit juice
5ml/1 tsp mixed spice
15ml/1 tbsp cider vinegar
sprigs of rosemary

1 If you prefer a smoked joint, be sure to soak it for at least 2 hours, or overnight first. Drain well.

2 Place the joint in a large pan with the cider, and add fresh water to cover. Add the cinnamon and peppercorns. Bring to the boil and simmer until cooked, allowing 20 minutes per 450g/1lb and about 20 minutes over.

3 Preheat the oven to 200°C/400°F/ Gas 6. Drain the joint (saving the liquid), cool slightly, then cut away the skin neatly with a sharp knife. Score the fat, in diamonds, then coat with 30–60ml/2–4 tbsp of the redcurrant jelly. Transfer to a roasting tin and bake for 10 minutes until golden brown.

4 Meanwhile, make the spiced peaches. Place 150ml/¼ pint/⅔ cup of the ham cooking liquid in a pan with the peach juice, the mixed spice, vinegar and 30ml/2 tbsp of the redcurrant jelly. Simmer for 10–15 minutes until syrupy. Add the peach slices and heat through. Serve hot with the ham, garnished with sprigs of rosemary.

--- COOK'S TIP ---

If you want a quicker serving accompaniment, choose a tasty fruit chutney, or buy ready prepared spiced peaches or pears.

DINNER PARTY DISHES

The best recipes for entertaining are relatively easy to make, yet look and taste fantastic. Sizzling Chinese Steamed Fish certainly fits the bill and is well worth trying out. Other fish dishes such as Salmon with Watercress Sauce, and Sole with Cider and Cream would be equally good. While, if you would prefer a meaty main course, Mexican Spiced Roast Leg of Lamb, or Peppered Steaks with Madeira are certain to please.

Chinese Omelettes with Fried Rice

Ingredients

Makes 4

30ml/2 tbsp sesame oil
30ml/2 tbsp sesame seeds
225g/8oz/1¼ cups cooked long grain rice
5cm/2in piece of cucumber, finely grated
5ml/1 tsp finely grated lemon rind
squeeze of lemon juice
6 eggs
15ml/1 tbsp dry sherry
15ml/1 tbsp light soy sauce
pinch of caster sugar
225g/8oz/2 cups cooked peeled prawns
4 spring onions, finely chopped
2 large tomatoes, seeded and chopped
30ml/2 tbsp vegetable oil
salt and black pepper
4 cooked prawns in shells and fresh coriander sprigs, to garnish

1 Heat the sesame oil in a pan and fry the sesame seeds until golden. Stir in the cooked rice, followed by the cucumber, lemon rind and juice and seasoning. Cook for 2–3 minutes, then keep warm while making the omelettes.

2 Place the eggs, sherry, soy sauce, sugar and a little pepper into a bowl and beat with a fork. Stir in the peeled prawns, spring onions and tomatoes.

3 Heat 7.5ml/½ tbsp of the oil in frying pan and ladle in a quarter of the mixture. Fry over a moderate heat for 3–4 minutes, until the omelette is lightly golden underneath. Cover and cook until the omelette is just set.

4 Remove the lid and fold the omelette in half. Garnish with a prawn and fresh coriander and serve with a spoonful of the rice. Make the remaining omelettes in the same way.

Sizzling Chinese Steamed Fish

Steamed whole fish is very popular in China and the wok is used as a steamer. In this recipe the fish is flavoured with garlic, fresh root ginger and spring onions cooked in sizzling hot oil.

Ingredients

Serves 4

4 rainbow trout (about 250g/9oz each)
1.25ml/¼ tsp salt
2.5ml/½ tsp sugar
2 garlic cloves, finely chopped
15ml/1 tbsp finely diced fresh root ginger
5 spring onions, cut into 5cm/2in lengths and finely shredded
60ml/4 tbsp groundnut oil
5ml/1 tsp sesame oil
45ml/3 tbsp light soy sauce
thread egg noodles, to serve

1 Make three diagonal slits on both sides of each fish and lay them on a heatproof plate. Place a small rack or trivet in a wok or large frying pan half filled with water, cover and heat until just simmering.

2 Sprinkle the fish with the salt, sugar, garlic and ginger. Sit the plate on the rack and cover. Steam gently for about 10–12 minutes, or until the flesh has turned pale pink and feels quite firm.

3 Turn off the heat, remove the lid and scatter the spring onions over the fish. Replace the lid.

4 Heat the oils in a small pan over a high heat until just smoking, then quickly pour a quarter over the spring onions on each of the fish – the shredded onions will sizzle and cook in the hot oil – then sprinkle the soy sauce over the top. Serve the fish and juices immediately with boiled noodles.

Baked Cod with Tomatoes

For the very best flavour, use firm ripe tomatoes for the sauce and make sure it is thick before spooning over the cod.

INGREDIENTS

Serves 4
30ml/2 tbsp olive oil
1 onion, chopped
2 garlic cloves, finely chopped
450g/1lb tomatoes, peeled, seeded and chopped
5ml/1 tsp tomato purée
60ml/4 tbsp dry white wine
60ml/4 tbsp chopped flat leaf parsley
4 cod cutlets
30ml/2 tbsp dried breadcrumbs
salt and black pepper
new potatoes and green salad, to serve

1 Preheat the oven to 190°C/375°F/ Gas 5. Heat the oil in a pan and fry the onion for about 5 minutes. Add the garlic, tomatoes, tomato purée, wine and seasoning. Bring just to the boil, then reduce the heat slightly and cook, uncovered, for 15–20 minutes until thick. Stir in the parsley.

2 Place the cod cutlets in a shallow greased ovenproof dish and spoon an equal quantity of the tomato sauce on to each piece. Sprinkle the dried breadcrumbs over the top.

3 Bake for 20–30 minutes, basting occasionally, until the breadcrumbs are golden and crisp. Serve with new potatoes and a green salad.

Sole with Cider and Cream

INGREDIENTS

Serves 4
50g/2oz/4 tbsp butter
1 onion, chopped
8 lemon sole fillets, about 115g/4oz each, skinned
300ml/½ pint/1¼ cups dry cider
150ml/¼ pint/⅔ cup fish stock
few parsley stalks
115g/4oz button mushrooms, sliced
115g/4oz cooked, peeled prawns, defrosted if frozen
15ml/1 tbsp each plain flour and butter, blended together to make a beurre manié
120ml/4fl oz/½ cup double cream
salt and black pepper
chopped fresh parsley, to garnish

1 Melt 25g/1oz/2 tbsp of the butter in a frying pan with a lid. Add the chopped onion and fry gently, stirring occasionally, until softened.

2 Lightly season the fish, then fold each into three. Place the fish in the pan, and pour over the cider and stock. Tuck in the parsley stalks. Bring to simmering point, cover and cook for 7–10 minutes, until the fish is tender.

3 Meanwhile, melt the remaining butter and cook the mushrooms in a separate pan until tender. Transfer the fish to a warmed serving plate and scatter over the prawns. Cover and keep warm while making the sauce.

4 Strain the fish cooking juices and return to the pan. Boil rapidly until slightly reduced. Add the beurre manié a little at a time, stirring until the sauce has thickened. Stir in the cream and seasoning to taste, then heat gently.

5 Spoon the cooked mushrooms over the fish, then pour over the cream sauce. Sprinkle with chopped fresh parsley and serve at once.

Mediterranean Fish Stew

INGREDIENTS

Serves 4

225g/8oz/2 cups cooked prawns in shells
450g/1lb mixed white fish fillets such as cod, whiting, haddock, mullet or monkfish skinned and chopped (reserve skins for the stock)
45ml/3 tbsp olive oil
1 onion, chopped
1 leek, sliced
1 carrot, diced
1 garlic clove, chopped
2.5ml/½ tsp ground turmeric
150ml/¼ pint/⅔ cup dry white wine or cider
400g/14oz can chopped tomatoes
sprig of fresh parsley, thyme and fennel
1 bay leaf
a small piece of orange peel
1 prepared squid, body cut into rings and tentacles chopped
12 mussels in shells
salt and black pepper
30–45ml/2–3 tbsp Parmesan cheese shavings, to sprinkle
chopped fresh parsley, to garnish

For the rouille sauce
2 slices white bread, crusts removed
2 garlic cloves, crushed
½ fresh red chilli
15ml/1 tbsp tomato purée
45–60ml/3–4 tbsp olive oil

1 Peel the prawns leaving the tails on; cover and chill. Place all the prawn trimmings and fish trimmings in a pan and cover with 450ml/¾ pint/1⅞ cups water. Bring to the boil, then cover and simmer for about 30 minutes. Strain and reserve the stock.

2 Heat the oil in a large saucepan and add the onion, leek, carrot and garlic. Fry gently for 6–7 minutes, then stir in the turmeric. Pour on the white wine, tomatoes and juice, the reserved fish stock, the herbs and orange peel. Bring to the boil, then cover and simmer gently for about 20 minutes.

3 Meanwhile, prepare the rouille sauce. Blend the bread in a food processor with the garlic, chilli and tomato purée. With the motor running, pour in the oil in a thin drizzle until the mixture is smooth and thickened.

4 Add the fish and seafood to the pan and simmer for 5–6 minutes, or until the fish is opaque and the mussels open. Remove the bay leaf and peel. Season the stew and serve in bowls with a spoonful of the rouille sauce, and sprinkled with Parmesan and parsley.

Salmon with Watercress Sauce

Fresh watercress gives the sauce a wonderful colour.

INGREDIENTS

Serves 4

300ml/½ pint/1¼ cups crème fraîche
30ml/2 tbsp chopped fresh tarragon
25g/1oz/2 tbsp unsalted butter
15ml/1 tbsp sunflower oil
4 salmon fillets, skinned and boned
1 garlic clove, crushed
100ml/3½fl oz/½ cup dry white wine
1 bunch watercress
salt and black pepper

1 Gently heat the crème fraîche in a small pan until just beginning to boil. Remove the pan from the heat and stir in half the tarragon. Leave the herb cream to infuse while cooking the fish.

2 Heat the butter and oil in a frying pan, add the salmon and fry for 3–5 minutes on each side. Remove from the pan and keep warm.

3 Add the garlic and fry for 1 minute, then pour in the wine and let it bubble until reduced to about 15ml/1 tbsp.

4 Meanwhile, strip the leaves off the watercress stalks and chop finely. Discard any damaged leaves. (Save the watercress stalks for soup, if you like.)

5 Strain the herb cream into the pan and cook for a few minutes, stirring until the sauce has thickened. Stir in the remaining tarragon and watercress, then cook for a few minutes, until wilted but still bright green. Season and serve at once, spooned over the salmon.

Middle Eastern Lamb Kebabs

Skewered, grilled meats are the main item in many Middle Eastern and Greek restaurants. In this recipe marinated lamb is grilled with vegetables.

INGREDIENTS

Makes 4

450g/1lb boneless leg of lamb, cubed
75ml/5 tbsp olive oil
15ml/1 tbsp chopped fresh oregano or thyme, or 10ml/2 tsp dried oregano
15ml/1 tbsp chopped fresh parsley
juice of ½ lemon
½ small aubergine, thickly sliced and quartered
4 baby onions, halved
2 tomatoes, quartered
4 fresh bay leaves
salt and black pepper
pitta bread and natural yogurt, to serve

1 Place the lamb in a bowl. Mix together the olive oil, oregano, parsley, lemon juice and seasoning, pour over the lamb and mix well. Cover and marinate for about 1 hour.

2 Preheat the grill. Thread the marinated lamb, aubergine, onions, tomatoes and bay leaves alternately on to four large skewers.

3 Place the kebabs on a grill rack and brush the vegetables liberally with the leftover marinade. Cook the kebabs under a medium heat for about 8–10 minutes on each side, basting once or twice with the juices that have collected in the bottom of the grill pan. Serve the kebabs hot, with hot pitta bread and natural yogurt.

COOK'S TIP

Make a lemony bulgur wheat salad to accompany the kebabs if you like. Or serve them with plain, boiled rice – either basmati or jasmine rice would be a good choice.

Mexican Spiced Roast Leg of Lamb

INGREDIENTS

Serves 4

1 small leg or half leg of lamb (about 1.25kg/2½lb)
15ml/1 tbsp dried oregano
5ml/1 tsp ground cumin
5ml/1 tsp hot chilli powder
2 garlic cloves
45ml/3 tbsp olive oil
30ml/2 tbsp red wine vinegar
salt and black pepper
fresh oregano sprigs, to garnish

1 Preheat the oven to 220°C/425°F/ Gas 7. Place the leg of lamb on a large chopping board.

2 Place the oregano, cumin, chilli powder and one of the garlic cloves, crushed, into a bowl. Pour on half of the olive oil and mix well to form a paste. Set the paste aside.

3 Using a sharp knife, make a criss-cross pattern of fairly deep slits through the skin and just into the meat.

4 Press the spice paste into the meat slits with the back of a knife.

5 Slice the remaining garlic clove thinly and cut each slice in half again. Push the pieces of garlic deeply into the slits in the meat (to prevent burning during roasting).

6 Mix the vinegar and remaining oil, pour over the joint and season with salt and freshly ground black pepper.

7 Bake for about 15 minutes at the higher temperature, then reduce the heat to 180°C/350°F/Gas 4 and cook for a further 1¼ hours (or a little longer if you like your meat well done). Serve the lamb with a delicious gravy made with the spicy pan juices and garnish with fresh oregano sprigs.

Peking Beef and Pepper Stir-fry

INGREDIENTS

Serves 4

350g/12oz rump or sirloin steak, sliced
  into strips
30ml/2 tbsp soy sauce
30ml/2 tbsp medium sherry
15ml/1 tbsp cornflour
5ml/1 tsp brown sugar
15ml/1 tbsp sunflower oil
15ml/1 tbsp sesame oil
1 garlic clove, finely chopped
15ml/1 tbsp grated fresh root ginger
1 red pepper, seeded and sliced
1 yellow pepper, seeded and sliced
115g/4oz sugar snap peas
4 spring onions, cut into 5cm/2in
  pieces
30ml/2 tbsp Chinese oyster sauce
hot noodles, to serve

1 In a bowl, mix together the steak strips, soy sauce, sherry, cornflour and brown sugar. Cover and leave to marinate for 30 minutes.

2 Heat the oils in a wok or large frying pan. Add the garlic and ginger and stir-fry quickly for about 30 seconds. Add the peppers, sugar snap peas and spring onions and stir-fry over a high heat for 3 minutes.

3 Add the beef with the marinade juices to the wok or frying pan and stir-fry for a further 3–4 minutes.

4 Finally, pour in the oyster sauce and 60ml/4 tbsp water and stir until the sauce has thickened slightly. Serve immediately with hot noodles.

Texan Barbecued Ribs

An American favourite of pork spare ribs cooked in a sweet and sour barbecue sauce. Ideal as a barbecue dish, this can be just as easily cooked in the oven and makes an excellent choice for a casual dinner party.

INGREDIENTS

Serves 4

1.5kg/3lb (about 16) lean pork spare
  ribs
1 onion, finely chopped
1 large garlic clove, crushed
120ml/4fl oz/½ cup tomato ketchup
30ml/2 tbsp orange juice
30ml/2 tbsp red wine vinegar
5ml/1 tsp mustard
10ml/2 tsp clear honey
30ml/2 tbsp soft light brown sugar
dash of Worcestershire sauce
30ml/2 tbsp vegetable oil
salt and black pepper
chopped fresh parsley, to garnish

1 Preheat the oven to 200°C/400°F/ Gas 6. Place the pork spare ribs in a large shallow roasting tin and bake for 20 minutes.

2 Meanwhile, mix together in a saucepan the onion, garlic, tomato ketchup, orange juice, wine vinegar, mustard, clear honey, brown sugar, Worcestershire sauce, oil and seasoning. Bring to the boil and simmer for about 5 minutes.

3 Remove the ribs from the oven and reduce the temperature to 180°C/ 350°F/Gas 4. Spoon over half the sauce, covering the ribs well and bake for 20 minutes. Turn them over, baste with the remaining sauce and cook for a further 25 minutes.

4 Sprinkle the ribs with parsley and serve three or four ribs per person. Provide small finger bowls for washing sticky fingers.

Breton Pork and Bean Casserole

INGREDIENTS

Serves 4

30ml/2 tbsp olive oil
1 onion, chopped
2 garlic cloves, chopped
450g/1lb lean shoulder of pork, cubed
340g/12oz lean lamb (preferably leg), cubed
225g/8oz coarse pork and garlic sausage, cut into chunks
400g/14oz can chopped tomatoes
30ml/2 tbsp red wine
15ml/1 tbsp tomato purée
bouquet garni
400g/14oz can cannellini beans, drained
50g/2oz/1 cup brown breadcrumbs
salt and black pepper
salad and French bread, to serve

1 Preheat the oven to 160°C/325°F/ Gas 3. Heat the oil in a large flameproof casserole and fry the onions and garlic until softened. Remove with a draining spoon and reserve.

2 Add the pork, lamb and sausage to the pan and fry on a high heat until browned on all sides. Return the onions and garlic to the pan.

3 Stir in the chopped tomatoes, wine and tomato purée and add 300ml/ ½ pint/1¼ cups water. Season well and pop in the bouquet garni.

4 Cover and bring to the boil, then transfer the casserole to the pre-heated oven and cook for 1½ hours.

5 Remove the bouquet garni, stir in the beans and sprinkle the bread-crumbs over the top. Return to the oven, uncovered, for a further 30 min-utes, until the top is golden brown. Serve hot with a green salad and French bread to mop up the juices.

----- COOK'S TIP -----

Replace the lamb with duck breast, if you like, but be sure to drain off any fat before sprinkling with the breadcrumbs.

Peppered Steaks with Madeira

A really easy special-occasion dish. Mixed dried peppercorns have an excellent flavour, though black pepper will, of course, do instead.

INGREDIENTS

Serves 4

15ml/1 tbsp mixed dried peppercorns (green, pink and black)
4 fillet or sirloin steaks, about 175g/6oz each
15ml/1 tbsp olive oil, plus extra for frying
1 garlic clove, crushed
60ml/4 tbsp Madeira
90ml/6 tbsp fresh beef stock
150ml/¼ pint/⅔ cup double cream
salt

1 Finely crush the peppercorns using a pestle and mortar, then press on to both sides of the steaks.

2 Place the steaks in a shallow non-metallic dish, then add the oil, garlic and Madeira. Cover and leave to marinate in a cool place for 4–6 hours, or preferably overnight.

3 Remove the steaks from the dish, reserving the marinade. Brush a little oil over a heavy-based frying pan and heat until hot.

4 Add the steaks and cook over a high heat, allowing 3 minutes per side for medium or 2 minutes per side for rare. Remove and keep warm.

5 Add the reserved marinade and the stock to the pan and bring to the boil, then leave the sauce to bubble until it is well reduced.

6 Add the cream, with salt to taste, to the pan and stir until slightly thickened. Serve the steaks on warmed plates with the sauce spooned over.

Ginger Pork with Black Bean Sauce

INGREDIENTS

Serves 4

350g/12oz pork fillet
1 garlic clove, crushed
15ml/1 tbsp grated fresh root ginger
90ml/6 tbsp chicken stock
30ml/2 tbsp dry sherry
15ml/1 tbsp light soy sauce
5ml/1 tsp sugar
10ml/2 tsp cornflour
45ml/3 tbsp groundnut oil
2 yellow peppers, seeded and cut into strips
2 orange peppers, seeded and cut into strips
1 bunch spring onions, diagonally sliced
45ml/3 tbsp preserved black beans, coarsely chopped
coriander sprigs, to garnish

1 Cut the pork into thin slices across the grain of the meat. Put the slices into a dish and mix them with the garlic and ginger. Leave to marinate at room temperature for 15 minutes.

2 Blend together the stock, sherry, soy sauce, sugar and cornflour in a small bowl, then set the sauce mixture aside.

3 Heat the oil in a wok or large frying pan, add the marinated pork and stir-fry for 2–3 minutes. Add the peppers and spring onions and stir-fry for a further 2 minutes.

4 Add the beans and sauce mixture and cook, stirring until thick. Serve hot, garnished with coriander.

Asparagus and Ham Gratin

Choose plump green asparagus spears and the best cooked ham for this tasty gratin – it's a good way of stretching a small quantity of asparagus! Serve with warm crusty bread.

INGREDIENTS

Serves 4

12 asparagus spears
6 slices roast ham, halved
40g/1½oz/3 tbsp butter
40g/1½oz/⅓ cup plain flour
450ml/¾ pint/1⅞ cups milk
10ml/2 tsp Dijon mustard
75g/3oz Gruyère cheese, grated
freshly grated nutmeg
25g/1oz Parmesan cheese, finely grated
25g/1oz/7 tbsp fresh fine white breadcrumbs
salt and black pepper

1 Preheat the oven to 190°C/375°F/ Gas 5. Trim the woody ends from the asparagus, then place the spears in a large frying pan with about 2.5cm/1in boiling water. Cover the pan and cook for 4 minutes, then drain thoroughly.

2 Wrap a slice of roast ham around each asparagus spear and arrange in a shallow buttered ovenproof dish.

3 Melt the butter in a pan. Add the flour and cook for 1 minute, stirring. Gradually add the milk, then bring to the boil, stirring to give a smooth sauce. Stir in the mustard, Gruyère, salt, pepper and nutmeg to taste.

4 Pour the sauce over the asparagus. Mix the Parmesan cheese with the breadcrumbs and sprinkle evenly over the top. Bake for about 20 minutes, until browned on top and bubbling. Serve immediately.

Pork with Mozzarella and Sage

Here is a variation of a famous Italian dish *Saltimbocca alla Romana* – the mozzarella adds a delicious creamy flavour.

INGREDIENTS

Serves 2–3
225g/8oz pork tenderloin
1 garlic clove, crushed
75g/3oz mozzarella cheese, cut into
 6 slices
6 slices Parma ham
6 large sage leaves
25g/1oz/2 tbsp unsalted butter
salt and black pepper
potato wedges roasted in olive oil, and
 green beans, to serve

1 Trim any excess fat from the pork, then cut the pork crossways into six pieces about 2.5cm/1in thick.

2 Stand each piece of tenderloin on end and bat down with a rolling pin to flatten. Rub with garlic and set aside for 30 minutes in a cool place.

3 Place a slice of mozzarella on top of each pork steak and season with salt and pepper. Lay a slice of Parma ham on top of each, crinkling it a little to fit.

4 Press a sage leaf on to each and secure with a cocktail stick. Melt the butter in a large heavy-based frying pan. Add the pork and cook for about 2 minutes on each side until you see the mozzarella melting. Remove the cocktail sticks and serve immediately with the potatoes and green beans.

Redcurrant-glazed Lamb Cutlets

Loin or chump chops could be used instead of the cutlets to make this dish more economical.

INGREDIENTS

Serves 4
8 lamb cutlets, about 2.5cm/1in thick
30ml/2 tbsp olive oil
30ml/2 tbsp red wine
½ garlic clove, chopped
60ml/4 tbsp redcurrant jelly
grated rind of 1 orange
30ml/2 tbsp chopped fresh mint
black pepper

1 Place the lamb cutlets in a shallow dish. To make the marinade, mix together the olive oil, red wine and garlic in a bowl, then season to taste with plenty of black pepper.

2 Pour the marinade over the meat, and leave to marinate for 1 hour.

3 Put the redcurrant jelly and orange rind in a small pan and stir over a low heat until the jelly melts. Remove from the heat and stir in the mint.

4 Lift the lamb cutlets from the marinade and arrange on a grill rack. Grill or barbecue for 10–15 minutes, according to whether you like your lamb rare or medium cooked, turning occasionally and brushing frequently with the redcurrant glaze.

Five-spice Lamb

INGREDIENTS

Serves 4

30–45ml/2–3 tbsp oil
1.5kg/3–3½lb leg of lamb, boned
 and cubed
1 onion, chopped
10ml/2 tsp grated fresh root ginger
1 garlic clove, crushed
5ml/1 tsp five-spice powder
30ml/2 tbsp hoisin sauce
15ml/1 tbsp light soy sauce
300ml/½ pint/1¼ cups passata
250ml/8fl oz/1 cup lamb stock
1 red pepper, seeded and cubed
1 yellow pepper, seeded and cubed
30ml/2 tbsp chopped fresh coriander
15ml/1 tbsp sesame seeds, toasted
salt and black pepper

1 Preheat the oven to 160°C/325°F/ Gas 3. Heat 30ml/2 tbsp of the oil in a flameproof casserole and brown the lamb in batches over a high heat. Remove and set aside.

2 Add the onion, ginger and garlic to the casserole with a little more of the oil, if necessary, and cook for about 5 minutes, until softened.

3 Return the lamb to the casserole. Stir in the five-spice powder, hoisin and soy sauces, passata, stock and seasoning. Bring to the boil, then cover and cook in the oven for 1¼ hours.

4 Remove the casserole from the oven, stir in the peppers, then cover and return to the oven for a further 15 minutes, or until the lamb is very tender.

5 Sprinkle with the coriander and sesame seeds. Serve hot.

Pork Steaks with Gremolata

Gremolata is a popular Italian dressing of garlic, lemon and parsley – it adds a hint of sharpness to the pork.

INGREDIENTS

Serves 4
30ml/2 tbsp olive oil
4 pork shoulder steaks
1 onion, chopped
2 garlic cloves, crushed
30ml/2 tbsp tomato purée
400g/14oz can chopped tomatoes
150ml/½ pint/⅔ cup dry white wine
bouquet garni
3 anchovy fillets, drained and chopped
salt and black pepper
salad leaves, to serve

For the gremolata
45ml/3 tbsp chopped fresh parsley
grated rind of ½ lemon
grated rind of 1 lime
1 garlic clove, chopped

1 Heat the oil in a large flameproof casserole, add the pork steaks and brown on both sides. Remove the steaks from the casserole.

2 Add the onion to the casserole and cook until soft and beginning to brown. Add the garlic and cook for 1–2 minutes, then stir in the tomato purée, chopped tomatoes and wine. Add the bouquet garni. Bring to the boil, then boil rapidly for 3–4 minutes to reduce and thicken slightly.

3 Return the pork to the casserole, then cover and cook for about 30 minutes. Stir in the chopped anchovies.

4 Cover the casserole and cook for a further 15 minutes, or until the pork is tender. Meanwhile, to make the gremolata, mix together the parsley, lemon and lime rinds and garlic.

5 Remove the pork steaks and discard the bouquet garni. Reduce the sauce over a high heat, if it is not already thick. Taste and adjust the seasoning.

6 Spoon the sauce over the pork, then sprinkle with the gremolata. Cover and cook for a further 5 minutes, then serve hot with salad leaves.

Pasta with Chicken Livers

INGREDIENTS

Serves 4

225g/8oz chicken livers, defrosted
   if frozen
30ml/2 tbsp olive oil
2 garlic cloves, crushed
175g/6oz smoked back bacon, rinded
   and roughly chopped
400g/14oz can chopped tomatoes
150ml/¼ pint/⅔ cup chicken stock
15ml/1 tbsp tomato purée
15ml/1 tbsp dry sherry
30ml/2 tbsp chopped fresh mixed herbs,
   such as parsley, rosemary and basil
350g/12oz dried orecchiette pasta
salt and black pepper
freshly grated Parmesan cheese,
   to serve

1 Wash and trim the chicken livers.
Cut into bite-sized pieces. Heat the
oil in a sauté pan and fry the chicken
livers for 3–4 minutes.

2 Add the garlic and bacon to the pan
and fry until golden brown. Add
the tomatoes, chicken stock, tomato
purée, sherry, herbs and seasoning.

3 Bring to the boil and simmer gently, uncovered, for about 5 minutes
until the sauce has thickened.

4 Meanwhile, cook the orecchiette
in boiling salted water for about 12
minutes until al dente. Drain well, then
toss into the sauce. Serve hot, sprinkled
with Parmesan cheese.

--- COOK'S TIP ---

You'll find *orecchiette*, a dried pasta shaped
like ears or flying saucers, in most large
supermarkets.

Chicken Baked in a Salt Crust

This unusual dish is extremely easy
to make. Once cooked, you just
break away the salt crust to reveal
the wonderfully tender, golden
brown chicken.

INGREDIENTS

Serves 4

1.5kg/3–3½lb corn-fed oven-ready
   chicken
bunch of mixed fresh herbs, such
   as rosemary, thyme, marjoram
   and parsley
about 1.5kg/3–3½lb/10 cups coarse sea
   salt
1 egg white
1–2 whole heads of baked garlic,
   to serve

1 Wipe the chicken and remove the
giblets. Put the herbs into the cavi-
ty, then truss the chicken.

2 Mix together the sea salt and egg
white until all the salt crystals are
moistened. Select a roasting tin into
which the chicken will fit neatly, then
line it with a large double layer of foil.

3 Spread a thick layer of moistened
salt in the foil-lined tin and place
the chicken on top. Cover with the
remaining salt and press into a neat
shape, over and around the chicken,
making sure it is completely enclosed.

4 Bring the foil edges up and over the
chicken to enclose it and bake in the
oven for 1½ hours. Remove from the
oven and leave to rest for 10 minutes.

5 Carefully lift the foil package from
the container and open. Break the
salt crust to reveal the chicken inside.
Brush any traces of salt from the bird,
then serve with baked whole heads of
garlic. Each clove can be slipped from
its skin and eaten with a bite of chicken.

Ruby Bacon Chops

This sweet, tangy sauce works well with lean bacon chops.

INGREDIENTS

Serves 4
1 pink grapefruit
4 lean boneless bacon chops
45ml/3 tbsp redcurrant jelly
black pepper

— COOK'S TIP —

Choose a really juicy grapefruit and make sure that you pare away all the white pith when you peel it, otherwise the sauce will be bitter.

1 Cut away all the peel and pith from the grapefruit, using a sharp knife, and carefully remove the segments, catching the juice in a bowl.

2 Cook the bacon chops in a non-stick frying pan without fat, turning them once, until golden and cooked.

3 Add the reserved grapefruit juice and redcurrant jelly to the pan and stir until melted. Add the grapefruit segments, then season with pepper, and serve hot with fresh vegetables.

Jamaican Bean Stew

If fresh pumpkin is not available, use any other type of squash, or try swede instead. This recipe is a good one to double – or even triple – for a crowd.

INGREDIENTS

Serves 4
450g/1lb stewing beef, diced
1 small pumpkin, about 450g/1lb, flesh diced
1 medium onion, chopped
1 green pepper, seeded and sliced
15ml/1 tbsp paprika
2 garlic cloves, crushed
2.5cm/1in piece fresh root ginger, chopped
400g/14oz can chopped tomatoes
115g/4oz baby corn cobs
250ml/8fl oz/1 cup beef stock
425g/15oz can chick-peas, drained
425g/15oz can red kidney beans, drained
salt and black pepper

1 Cook the diced beef without fat in a large flameproof casserole, stirring to seal it on all sides.

2 Stir in the pumpkin, onion, and pepper, cook for 2 minutes more, then add the paprika, garlic, and ginger.

3 Stir in the tomatoes, corn, and broth, then bring to a boil. Cover and simmer for 40–45 minutes or until tender. Add the chick-peas and beans, and heat thoroughly. Adjust the seasoning with salt and pepper to taste. Serve hot, with couscous or rice.

— VARIATION —

If there aren't any baby corn cobs available, then use a small can of sweetcorn instead. Add this to the stew with the chickpeas and beans.

INDEX